The BOYS' book of THINGS TO MAKE

A Dorling Kindersley Book

DK

LONDON, NEW YORK, MELBOURNE, MUNICH, AND DELHI

Editor James Mitchem
Senior Designer Sadie Thomas
Designers Charlotte Bull, Ria Holland, Poppy Joslin
Photography Andy Crawford
Additional editing Grace Redhead, Nikki Sims
Managing Editor Penny Smith
Managing Art Editor Marianne Markham
Category Publisher Mary Ling
Art Director Jane Bull
Production Editor Raymond Williams
Senior Production Controller Seyhan Esen
Jacket Designer Wendy Bartlet
Creative Technical Support Sonia Charbonnier

First published in Great Britain in 2013 by
Dorling Kindersley Limited, 80 Strand, London WC2R 0RL

A CIP catalogue record for this book is available from
the British Library

ISBN: 978-1-4093-2233-7

Printed and bound in China by South China Co. Ltd.
Discover more at www.dk.com

The BOYS' book of THINGS TO MAKE

Contents

Milk planets

Knight puppet

Come on, join the fun!

Soap monsters

Make it

Learn how to create **SOMETHING** out of **NOTHING.** Here, we'll show you how to make everything from a periscope to peer over walls, to scary alien masks, soap monsters, and much, much more. So, what are you waiting for? Turn the page now!

Move over Captain Jack Sparrow! Make way for your own pirate ships or naval fleet. Set these **QUICK-TO-MAKE SHIPS** to sail on a pond or a stream. And then see how quickly you can **SINK** the enemy's lot.

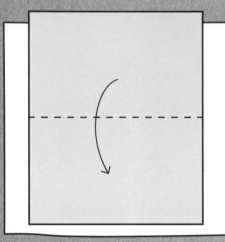

1 Take a rectangular sheet of coloured paper or card and fold it in half from top to bottom.

2 Fold the paper in half again to make a crease. Unfold it and fold the corners down to the centre.

You will need
- Large sheets of paper or card
- Flags

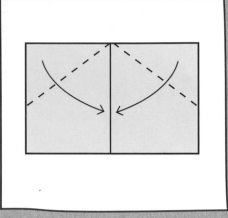

3 Take the front strip from the bottom, and fold it up over the dotted line shown here.

Grrrr

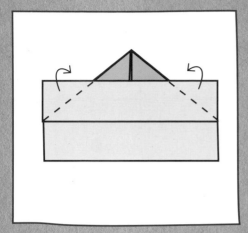

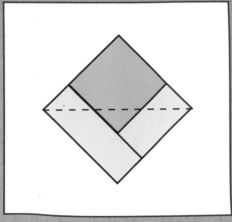

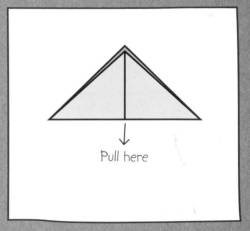

4 Fold the corners over the back, then turn the paper around and fold up the second strip.

5 Holding the middle of the strips, pull the paper outwards so that it looks like the square above.

6 Fold the strips up, one at the front, and one at the back, then pull the paper outwards as shown.

Decorate your ships with flags

7 You should have a shape like this. Pull the side triangles apart from the top to finish your boat.

Argh! Cannon ball attack!

Urban periscope

Submarines use periscopes to stay out of sight while checking out what's on the surface. You too can **PEEK OVER WALLS** and **AROUND CORNERS** without being seen using this handheld version. Perfect for budding secret agents!

You will need

- Two juice cartons
- Scissors
- Sticky tape
- Protractor
- Pencil
- Two plastic craft mirrors
- Paints, markers, and paper to decorate

1 Cut the tops off the juice cartons. Clean the cartons, then tape them together in the middle to form one long tube.

2 Cut a square hole near the bottom of the tube, then turn the tube upside down and cut another hole on the opposite side.

First square hole

Second square hole

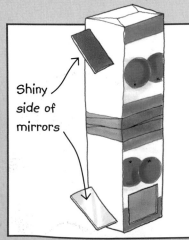

3 Put the tube on its side and use a protractor to mark a 45° angle sloping away from the square holes.

4 Cut out slits along the marks the same length as the mirrors. Slide in the mirrors so the shiny sides face each other, as shown.

Shiny side of mirrors

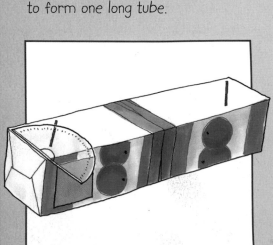

TOP TIP
Once you've made your periscope, decorate it with pens, paints, or wrapping paper.

HOW IT WORKS

Mirrors reflect almost all of the light that falls on them, and they only reflect it in one direction. The periscope reflects the light from one mirror to the other, and then into our eyes so we see the image.

Light enters the periscope here

The light is reflected from this mirror

This second mirror reflects the light into your eyes

Look through here

TOP TIP
Camouflage your periscope so that you can stay totally hidden.

Balloon drag racer

Make your own balloon-powered drag racing car using things you might find lying around the house. Why not **ORGANIZE A RACE** and ask your friends to build cars too? Who will be the winner?

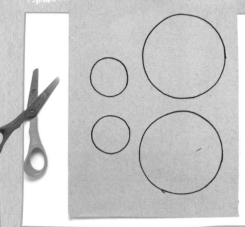

You will need
- Straw
- Sticky tape
- Plastic bottle
- Wooden skewers
- Cardboard
- Scissors
- Blu-tack
- Plastic tubing
- Balloon
- Rubber band

Make sure the straws are level

1 Cut the straw in half. Then firmly tape the two halves to the same side of the top and bottom of the plastic bottle.

2 Put the skewers through the straws. They need to be loose enough so that they can turn without getting stuck.

3 Draw around something circular on the cardboard for two large and two small wheels. Cut these out.

The tubing should be about 12cm (5in) long

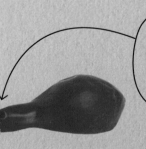

Make sure the rubber band doesn't cut off the air supply

4 Mark a dot in the middle of the wheels and poke the skewers through. Secure each wheel in place with the Blu-tack.

5 Insert the plastic tubing into the balloon and wrap the rubber band around it to keep it in place.

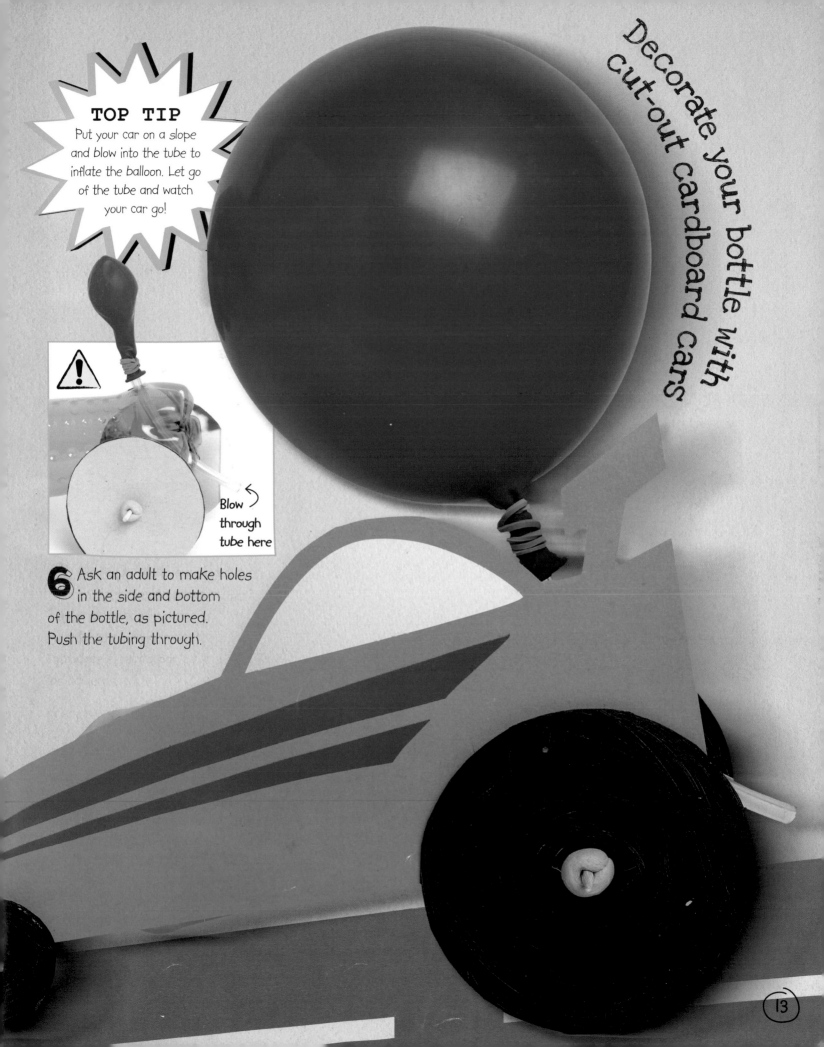

TOP TIP

Put your car on a slope and blow into the tube to inflate the balloon. Let go of the tube and watch your car go!

⚠

Blow through tube here

6 Ask an adult to make holes in the side and bottom of the bottle, as pictured. Push the tubing through.

You don't need a fancy kit or special glue to make a **COOL AEROPLANE.** Just learn the right sequence of folds to build **YOUR OWN FLYING MACHINE** – anytime, anywhere.

You will need
- Sheets of paper
- Paints
- Pens
- Stickers

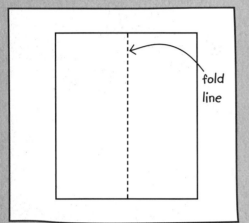

fold line

1 Fold the paper in half lengthways, then unfold it to create a line along the middle.

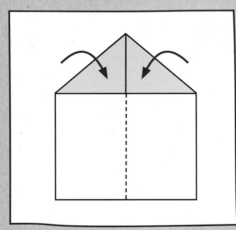

2 Fold two corners over towards the line to create a pointed top. Make sure they are the same size.

If the nose gets crumpled in a crash, the plane won't fly properly. You can protect the nose by folding it back on itself

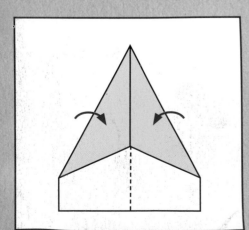

3 Neatly fold the sides in towards the middle. Flatten and smooth out all the folds.

4 Fold one side of the plane across the middle and lay the plane out flat.

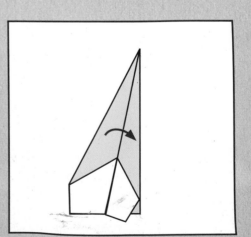

5 Fold one of the diagonal edges back along the straight side. Then repeat for the other side.

Crisp folds make the plane stiffer, which helps the plane to keep its shape

Fighter jet

Now, find some space and launch your plane!

If you lift one of the flaps slightly, your plane will fly in a spiral

Rocket

IN YOUR HANGAR

You can make your own squadron of planes and design how they look. Try different coloured paper, and add details and symbols with paint and stickers.

EXPERIMENT

Why not see if you can come up with other ways of making planes?

By folding in the nose, you can make your plane look like a flying fish

15

Recycled robots

Set your own **SCRAPHEAP CHALLENGE** and build a robot from junk or the recycling box. What **KINDS OF CHARACTERS** will you create?

Door stop

Sink drainer

1 Collect your materials and sketch out a design for your robots. Or just use this sketch of a robot head.

2 Attach the door stop to the sink drainer with glue, and then stick it to the tin can and leave it to dry.

Magnet

Bolt

3 Glue magnets to the can where you want the eyes, nose, and mouth, then attach bolts and screws.

Magnet

Circular items work well as eyes

Robot gallery

You can make robot characters out of almost anything: screws, brushes, tins, cutlery, hooks, bolts – whatever you can find! Just look for interesting parts and be creulive.

Old forks make good feet!

You will need

- Large milk carton
- Scissors
- Paper fasteners
- String
- Plastic bags
- Acrylic paints

Whether you want a **FUNKY WALL DECORATION** for your room or the start of a scary **HALLOWEEN OUTFIT**, these alien masks fit every bill. So, now to the task of sourcing the cartons. Glass of milk, anyone?

If you're making the masks as decorations, use a variety of different sized cartons

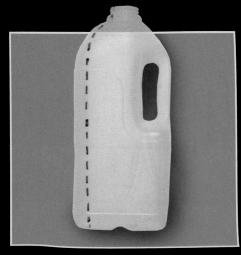

1 Mark a dotted line all the way around the front of the milk carton. Cut off the front side.

2 Next mark a line across the carton as shown above. Cut it off to make a detachable jaw.

Make a hole here

Make holes here

3 Draw and cut out the teeth and eyes. Poke two holes on either side where the head and jaw will meet, and two more behind the eyes.

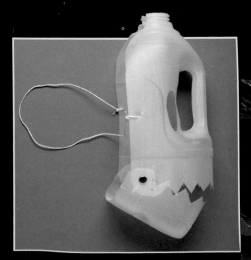

4 Insert the paper fasteners through the holes to attach the jaw and head, and poke string through the holes behind the eyes.

19

Secret book safe

The best hiding places are the least obvious. And what could be more **ORDINARY** than a book on a shelf? But even though this book is right under anyone's nose, it has a secret...

1 Dilute the glue with a little water. Open the book and, leaving a few pages untouched at the front, brush the sides with the glue.

Once dry, brush with glue again

2 Close the book and use some post it notes to separate the pages you saved. Weigh it down with another book until the glue dries.

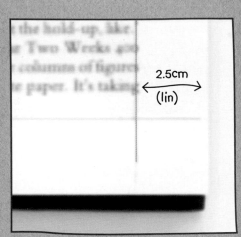

2.5cm (1in)

3 Open the book and fold back the saved pages. Using a ruler, draw a rectangle about 2.5cm (1in) from the edges on the next page.

4 Ask an adult to cut out the rectangle with a craft knife. It's dangerous, so don't try to do this yourself.

Make all the pages stick together

5 Brush the insides of the book with the glue and leave it to dry. You might need to do this a few times to get it to stick properly.

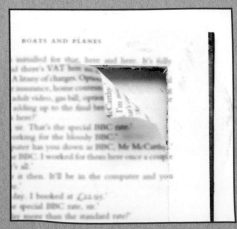

6 To neaten the cut edges, stick one of the spare pages over the top and trim just in from the sides.

Fill your book with
what you want to
hide and put it
back on the Shelf

Monster mirror

Get your friends round and *see* who can do the best **"I'M BEING EATEN BY A MONSTER"** face in this cool mirror. Funny faces and scary faces also allowed.

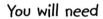

1 Draw the outline of your monster onto two pieces of cardboard and cut them out.

2 Cut out a hole in the middle of one of the pieces of cardboard, and draw on eyes and teeth.

Alien ships are good shapes for mirrors too!

3 Paint the outsides of both pieces of cardboard and leave them to dry.

4 Position the mirror so it covers the hole and the shiny side faces the front. Secure it with tape.

Eeek, help me! I'm squashed!

5 Glue the pieces together and weigh them down until they're dry.

Knight puppet

Recycle your rubbish to bring a knight TO LIFE. Now, what to call him? Sir Plus, perhaps?

Start here

1 Take a long piece of string. Tie a knot at one end and a safety pin to the other. Make a hole in the bottom of a cup and thread the end with the safety pin through from inside. Tape the knot to the inside of the cup.

2 Cut a kitchen roll tube in half and thread the string up through it. Repeat steps 1 and 2 to make the second leg.

3 Make two holes in the bottom of a soup carton and thread the string of each leg through.

4 Make a hole in either side of the soup carton. Tie knots in two new pieces of string and thread through each hole.

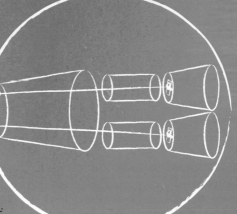

Musical instruments

Feeling like making some noise? Well, there's no need for expensive keyboards, guitars, or drum kits to **BANG OUT A TUNE**. Just lay your hands on some jars, tin cans, and the all-important spoon.

You will need

- Balloons
- Tin cans
- Rubber bands

Jar xylophone

Add water to some jars and you'll have a range of dings to play a tune. More water creates a deeper sound; less water makes it sound higher. Use different food colourings to keep track of which sounds are which.

You will need

- Empty jars
- Spoon
- Water
- Food colouring

Handheld bongos

1 Cut along the edge of a balloon so that you end up with a big, flat piece of rubbery material.

2 Stretch the balloon over the rim of a tin can and secure it very tightly with elastic bands.

3 Add and secure a second balloon. Cut tiny holes in the top balloon for decoration.

Beat out a rhythm!

TOP TIP
Use different-sized tins to produce a range of sounds on your homemade drum kit.

Milk planets

Our own galaxy – the Milky Way – has countless **STARS AND PLANETS** but you need a telescope to see them clearly. But did you know you can create **A SOLAR SYSTEM** of planets in your own kitchen? Here's how.

You will need
- Jar lids
- Milk
- Food colouring
- Washing-up liquid
- Cotton buds

Look at me. I'm in space!

1 Turn the jar lids upside down on a table top and fill them with a little milk. You need enough to just cover the bottom.

2 Add a few drops of different food colourings to the milk. Use as many colours as you like to make them look interesting.

3 Dip the cotton bud into the washing-up liquid, then use it to swirl the milk and food colouring into planet-like patterns.

Pizza dough

Everyone loves pizza. And the tastiest pizzas use **HOMEMADE DOUGH**. Here's how to make it.

You will need

- 500g (1lb, 2oz) strong white flour
- 10g (¼oz) sachet of dried yeast
- Salt
- 360ml (12fl oz) warm water
- 4 tbsp olive oil

1 Put the yeast and warm water in a bowl. Mix together with your finger, then leave for 5 minutes.

2 Mix the flour and oil in another bowl. Make a well in the centre, add the yeast mixture and stir.

3 Put some flour on your hands and knead the dough for 10 minutes. Ask an adult to show you how to do it.

4 Put the dough into a bowl and cover with clingfilm. Leave it in a warm place for about 30 minutes, or until it has doubled in size.

5 Push your fist into the dough to knock out any excess air. Knead it one more time then gather your toppings.

This should make enough for four pizzas

Turn the
page for
topping
ideas...

Pizza party

You will need

- Dough (*see pages 30–31*)
- Plain flour
- Tomato purée or passata
- Cheddar or mozzarella cheese

Topping ideas

- Mushrooms
- Peppers
- Olives
- Pepperoni
- Basil/oregano
- Sweetcorn
- Ham
- Cooked chicken
- Tomatoes

One of the *best* things about making pizza is that you can add **ALMOST ANY TOPPING** you want and it will pretty much **ALWAYS TASTE DELICIOUS**! Invite your friends over to try out and rate different flavour combinations.

Pick me! I'm delicious on pizzas!

1 Preheat the oven to 220°C (425°F). Scatter a little flour on a board and a rolling pin, then roll out the dough into 18cm (7in) discs.

2 Put a big dollop of the passata or tomato purée onto the middle of each *base* and spread it around with the back of a spoon.

3 Choose combinations of your favourite toppings and layer them onto the pizza *bases*. Make faces if you like.

4 Sprinkle grated cheddar or torn mozzarella on top, and bake the pizzas in the oven for 10–12 minutes, or until golden brown.

TOP TIP
Use torn or grated cheese. It'll melt more evenly than chunks of cheese.

why not make funny faces with the toppings?

Pick 'n' mix cookies

If you're starving after school, you can make and bake these cookies in under half an hour. And you can **CHANGE THE FLAVOUR** in a single step. Now, what flavour for today? Chocolate? Nutty? Smarties on top? You choose.

You will need

- 100 g (3½ oz) butter, at room temperature
- 1 egg
- 125 g (4½ oz) caster sugar
- ½ tsp vanilla extract
- 150 g (5½ oz) self-raising flour
- Chocolate chips, nuts, raisins, and glacé cherries

1 Preheat the oven to 180°C (350°F). Mix the butter, egg, sugar, and vanilla together in a mixing bowl, using a whisk.

2 Sieve in the flour, and stir the mixture until it's a smooth dough. Add in chocolate chips, or your other chosen flavouring here.

3 Roll the dough into balls and flatten them slightly. Place on a baking tray, leaving space around each cookie. Bake for 15 minutes.

Raisins

Chocolate chips

Add ingredients at stage 2 if you want different flavours

Walnuts

Fancy an ice-cold milk shake on a hot day? Well, they're **QUICK TO MAKE** and any flavours go, pretty much. So, just decide on the **FLAVOUR COMBINATION**, get the ingredients together, and press the on button. What could be simpler? (Serves 4).

You will need

- 400g (14oz) mixed red berries, 4 bananas, or other fruit of your choice
- 600ml (1 pint) milk
- 8 scoops vanilla ice cream

1 Prepare your fruit by removing stalks from strawberries, peeling bananas, or removing stones from peaches. When you're done, put the fruit in the blender.

2 Add the milk and ice cream and blend it all together for a minute or so. Pour the mixture into glasses and serve. Yum!

Mango

Raspberries

Peach

Strawberries

Chocolate

Banana

TOP TIP
Experiment with different ingredients and see which you like best. The great thing about milk shakes is that most fruits work well, and you can add chocolate, too!

Glow-in-the-dark jelly

Take jelly to a whole new level by using **A SPECIAL INGREDIENT** – tonic water – to make it glow under UV light. Perfect for a Halloween party.

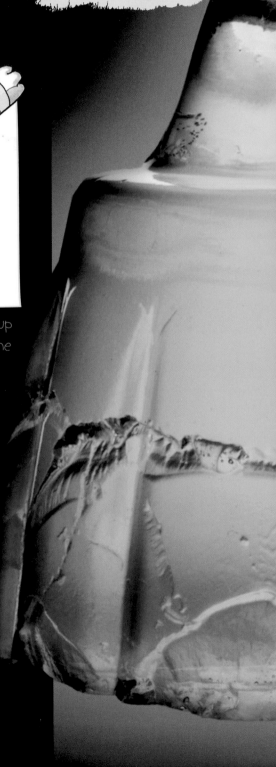

1 Follow the instructions on the jelly packet, but use tonic water instead of regular water.

2 If the instructions say to, top up the jelly. Add sugar to make the jelly taste less bitter.

3 Pour the mixture into a jelly mould or bowl and put it in the refrigerator to set.

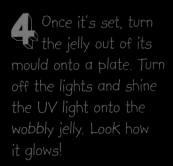

4 Once it's set, turn the jelly out of its mould onto a plate. Turn off the lights and shine the UV light onto the wobbly jelly. Look how it glows!

Tonic water contains a substance called QUININE, which causes the jelly to glow

TOP TIP
Inexpensive UV lights can be found in most hardware shops or on the Internet.

Erupting volcano

Be an amateur vulcanologist from the safety of your own kitchen. Make this smaller-than-normal **TABLE-TOP VOLCANO** and watch the **LAVA** erupt from its summit.

You will need

- Plastic bottle
- 3 tbsp baking soda
- Red food colouring
- Washing-up liquid
- Sand
- Vinegar

1 Fill the bottle about three-quarters full with warm water. Add the baking soda and mix together until dissolved.

2 Add a few drops of red food colouring, pop the lid on, and shake until mixed. Then add a drop of washing-up liquid.

3 Pile damp sand around the bottle to make it look like a volcano. If you prefer, you can use papier mâché instead.

4 Pour vinegar into your volcano. Sit back and watch the red lava flow!

REAL VOLCANOES don't work the same way. Your volcano erupts because the baking soda and vinegar cause a reaction when they're mixed. A real volcano erupts when molten rock (magma) forces its way up from the ground under massive pressure.

Argh, run away!

Soap monsters

You will need

- Bars of soap
- Plate
- Microwave
- Paperclips, googly eyes, pipe cleaners, and ring pulls

Did you know that your microwave can be **A MONSTER FACTORY?** Follow these instructions to create your own family of crazy monsters.

Once the monsters are fully cooled, decorate them in funny ways

Take a bar of soap and put in on a plate. Ask an adult to microwave it on the highest setting for two minutes. Let it cool down before taking it out of the microwave, as it will be very hot.

Meet my family

HOW IT WORKS

The heat from the microwave causes water molecules in the soap to form bubbles, which expand, causing the bars of soap to grow.

42

My brother Max

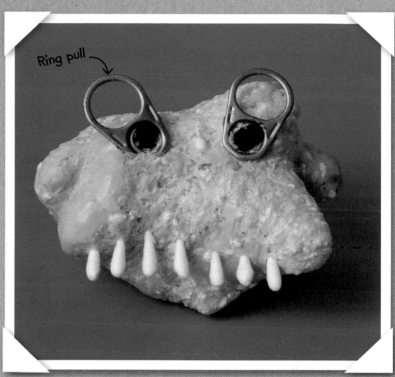

Ring pull

Dad

My brother Norman

Mum

Try using different colour soaps for a multicoloured family

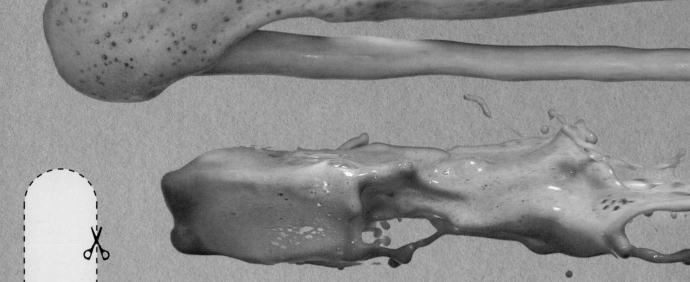

Soda fountain

What happens when you mix a mint with a fizzy drink? Something **VERY VERY MESSY**. After trying this experiment, you'll never want to eat them at the same time again!

You will need

- Bottles of fizzy drink
- Card
- A toothpick
- Sugar-coated mints

1 Roll up a piece of card. Put the card in the neck of a bottle of fizzy drink.

2 Push a toothpick through the card so it rests on the rim of the bottle. Drop a few mints on top.

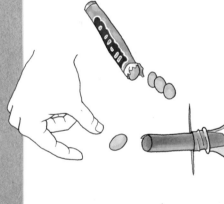

3 When you're ready, pull out the toothpick so the mints fall into the bottle. Quickly pull out the cardboard tube, stand back and watch the drink shoot into the air!

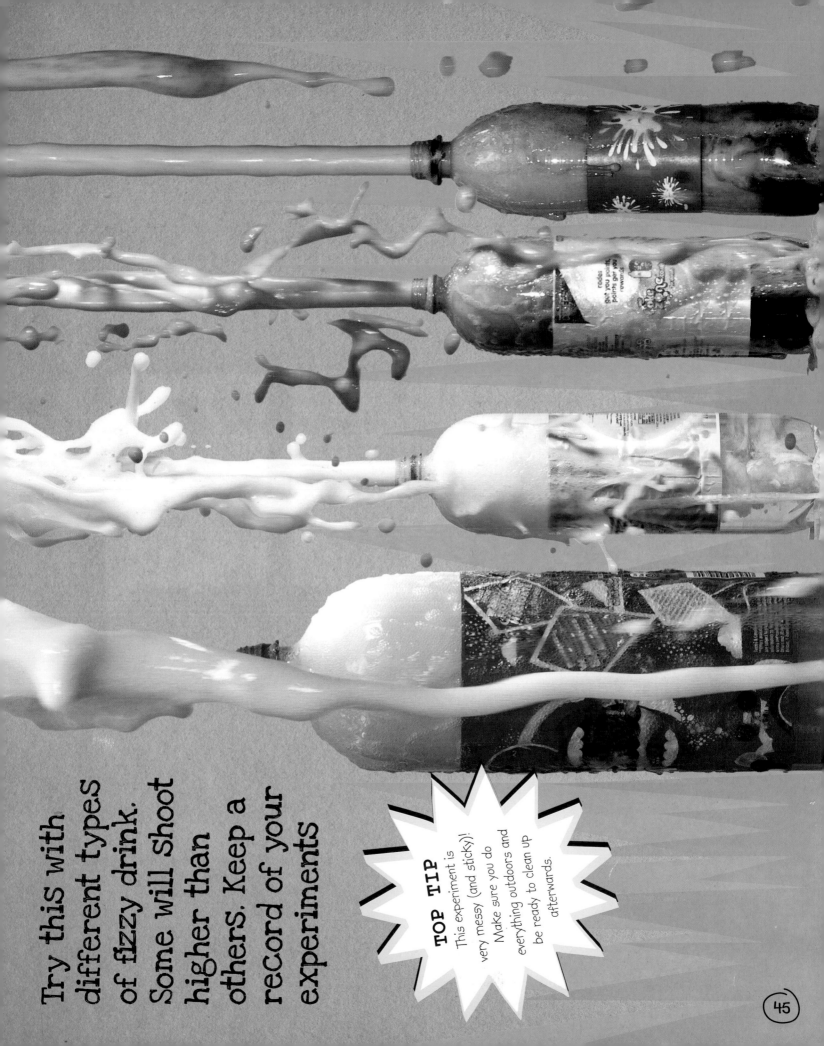

Try this with different types of fizzy drink. Some will shoot higher than others. Keep a record of your experiments

TOP TIP
This experiment is very messy (and sticky)! Make sure you do everything outdoors and be ready to clean up afterwards.

45

Make your own slime

IS SLIME A SOLID OR A LIQUID? It's actually both. Strictly it's a non-Newtonian fluid, which means that although it's a liquid, it can behave like a solid. Make a batch and see for yourself.

1 Fill a mug with cornflour and pour it into a mixing bowl.

2 Add half a glass of water and stir it all together.

3 Add a few drops of food colouring and mix together.

What can you do with your slime?

Try stretching it out or rolling it into a ball

46

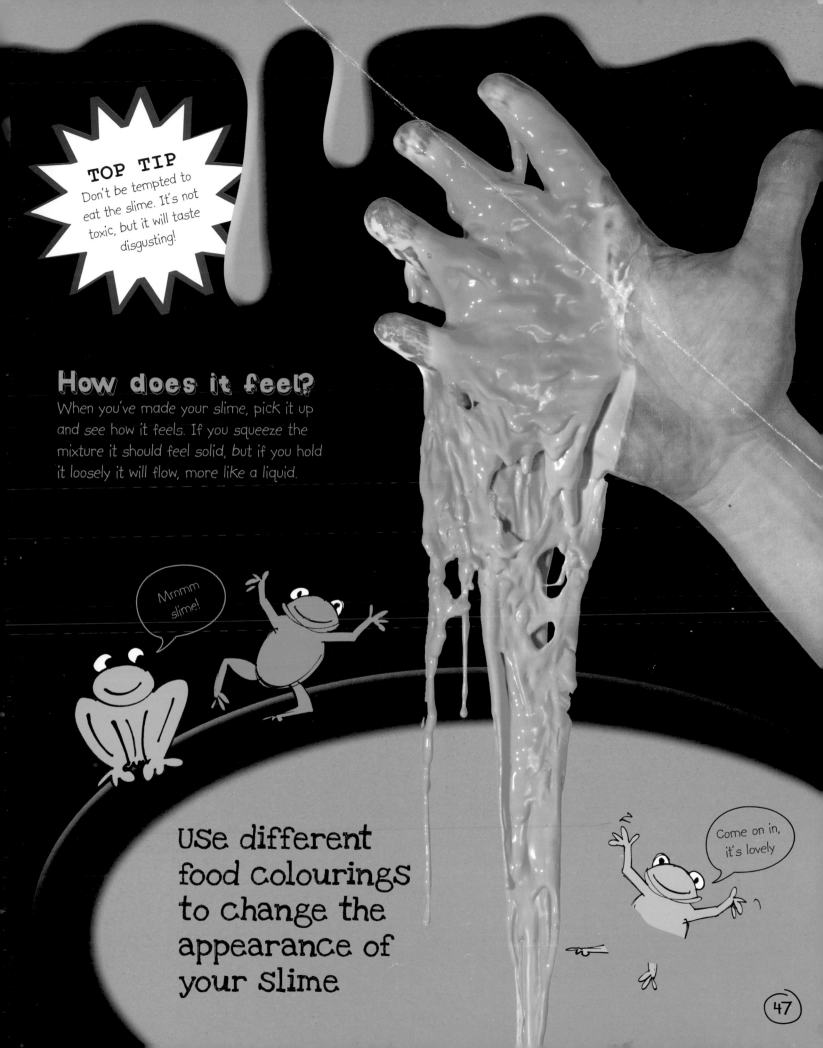

How does it feel?

When you've made your slime, pick it up and see how it feels. If you squeeze the mixture it should feel solid, but if you hold it loosely it will flow, more like a liquid.

Mrnmm slime!

Use different food colourings to change the appearance of your slime

Come on in, it's lovely

47

Launch a bottle rocket

While your back garden might not rival NASA's Cape Canaveral for **ROCKET LIFT-OFF**, you can use a similar scientific principle to launch a bottle-sized rocket of your own.

You will need

- Foot pump
- Cork
- Card
- Empty plastic bottle
- Water
- Tape

1 Push the needle adaptor from the pump all the way through the cork. You will probably need an adult to help you.

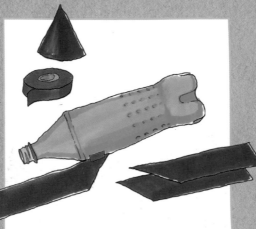

2 Cut four fins for your rocket from the card. Turn the bottle upside down and tape the fins on so they stand up, making sure to leave enough room underneath for the pump.

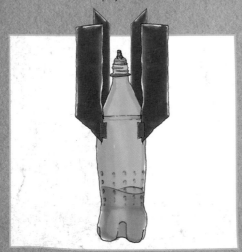

3 Fill the bottle one-quarter full with water. Push the cork in. It should be a really tight fit. If it isn't, take it out and wrap tape around it.

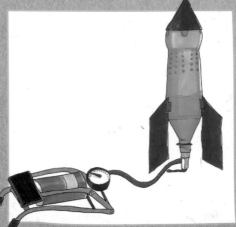

4 Stand the bottle up and attach the pump to the needle. Place the bottle as far away from the pump as possible.

5 Get everybody to stand well back and get an adult to start pumping, so you'll have the best view for lift-off.

HOW IT WORKS
When you pump air into the bottle (you'll see the bubbles in the water), it increases the air pressure inside the bottle. Once the air pressure inside becomes high enough, it forces out the cork, releasing the water and launching the bottle rocket high into the air.

A camera obscura (darkened room) is a box that projects an **UPSIDE-DOWN IMAGE** of the object in front of it, through a tiny pinhole. It's an ancient device, but it led to the invention of the **CAMERA**! Here's how to make one.

TOP TIP
Your subject needs to be well lit to produce a sharp image. Try pointing your camera at something outdoors, or near a window.

I'm ready for my close up!

You will need

- Empty cube-shaped tissue box
- Kitchen roll tube
- Coloured tissue paper
- Magnifying glass
- Tape
- Tracing paper

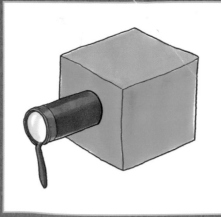

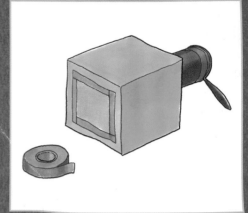

1 Take the tissue box and on the opposite side of the opening, draw around the end of the kitchen roll tube. Cut the hole out.

2 Decorate the box with tissue paper, making sure no light gets in. Tape the magnifying glass to the end of the kitchen roll tube and push the other end into the box.

3 Cut a sheet of tracing paper and tape it to the opening of the box. It needs to be stretched very flat, with no creases.

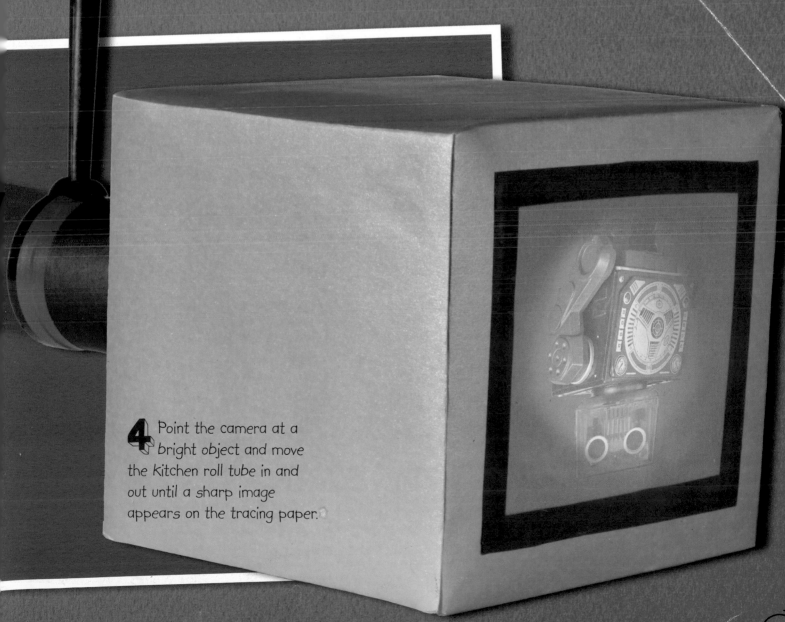

4 Point the camera at a bright object and move the kitchen roll tube in and out until a sharp image appears on the tracing paper.

Do it

Whether you're cooped up on a **RAINY DAY**, want something new to do outdoors, or fancy learning a **NEW TRICK**, this section has plenty of activities and games to keep you entertained all year. So, what are you waiting for? **LET'S GET TO IT!**

Wild-West cacti garden

With just a little bit of green-fingered magic and some imagination, you can recreate an **AMERICAN FRONTIER** in a mini garden. Just watch out for the **ARROWS**!

You will need
- Shallow pot
- Gravel
- Cactus potting mix
- Gloves
- Sand and toys

1 Put a layer of gravel into the shallow pot. Cover it with a 2.5cm (1in) layer of cactus potting mix, leaving holes for the cacti.

2 Add the cacti to the tray and push soil around their bases with a spoon. Be sure to wear thick gloves so you don't get prickled!

3 Cacti don't need a lot of water, which is how they survive in harsh desert environments. So, just lightly mist the soil every few days.

Attack!

GIGANTIC CACTI
Did you know that the giant Saguaro cactus found in Arizona, USA, can grow to be more than 20m (70ft) tall!

TOP TIP
The best place for your cacti garden is somewhere shady and warm.

Decorate your garden with sand paths and toys to give it that wild-west feel

Fingerprint doodles

Raining outside? If your day trip plans change because of the weather, why not **TRANSPORT YOURSELF SOMEWHERE ELSE** anyway. All you need is paper, ink, a pen, and 10 fingers and it's next stop the beach, farm, or space.

You will need

- Inkpad or paints
- Paper or notebook
- Pens and pencils
- Decorations

1 Press your finger on to the inkpad, or dip it into paint. Roll your finger onto the paper. Use different fingers for different sized prints.

2 Wait until the ink has dried and draw on details (arms, legs, and eyes) to transform the prints into characters. Add speech bubbles, too.

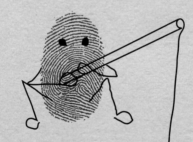

Thumb print

Little finger print

56

DIY crazy golf

Crazy golf is a great way to spend an afternoon but it's not something you can do whenever you want. Or is it? Well, with a little know-how, you can **PLAY A ROUND** in the comfort of your home.

You will need

- Kitchen roll tube
- Boxes and other rubbish
- Card
- Wooden skewer
- A can
- Plasticine
- Golf club and ball

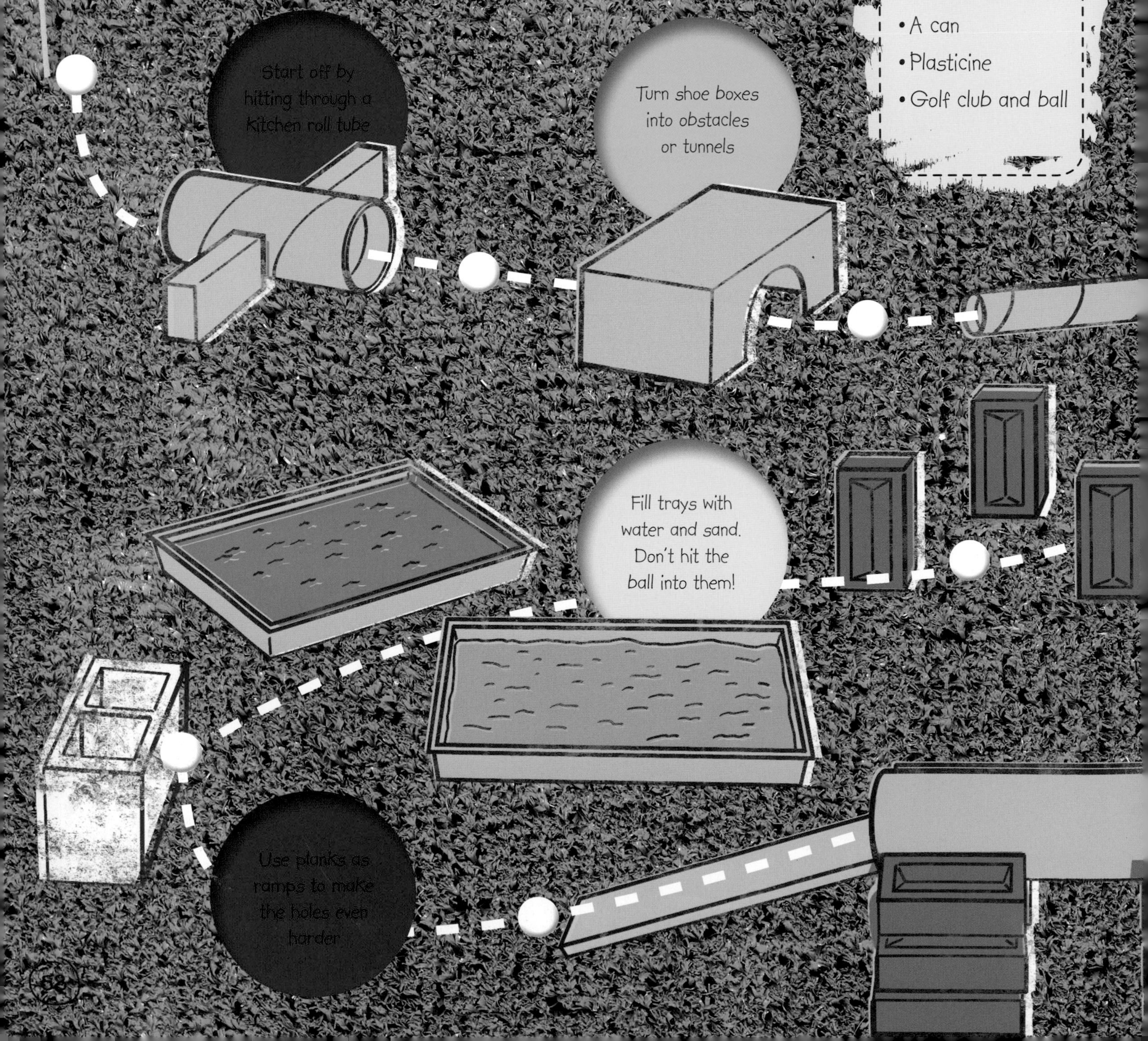

Start off by hitting through a kitchen roll tube

Turn shoe boxes into obstacles or tunnels

Fill trays with water and sand. Don't hit the ball into them!

Use planks as ramps to make the holes even harder

HOW TO PLAY

1. Use bricks, wood, and cardboard to make some courses. Try to make each one different. Each course needs a hole and a starting point.

2. Try to get the ball in the hole in the fewest number of shots. The player with the lowest score wins.

A hole in 1, 2, 3

No golf course is complete without holes. So, our crazy golf course uses these little holes, whether you're indoors or out.

Use a wrapping paper tube as a super-long tunnel

Planks of wood can become walls to bounce your shots off

Stack up bricks and try to weave the ball in between them

Put the hardest obstacle at the end of the course!

1 Cut out pieces of card in the shape of a triangle, and stick them to a wooden skewer or piece of bamboo with some tape.

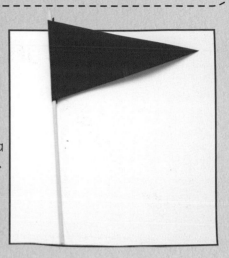

2 Wrap a can with anything you like: astroturf, wrapping paper, or even newspaper. Be careful of the sharp edges.

3 Stick your flag to the hole and put plasticine at the base to keep the can steady. Now, you're ready to tee-off!

Trick your taste buds

Did you know it's easy to fool your taste buds with the **RIGHT MIX OF CHEMICALS**. This delicious apple pie is missing one important ingredient – **APPLES!** Make it and see if your friends can tell.

1 Roll out half the ready-made pastry, and line the pie dish with it. Evenly scatter the crumbled crackers in the lined pie dish.

2 Heat the water, sugar, and cream of tartar in a saucepan. Simmer for 15 minutes and then stir in the lemon zest, juice, and cinnamon. Leave to cool.

3 Pour the cooled syrup over the filling and dot with chunks of butter. Ask an adult to preheat the oven to 220°C (425°F/Gas 7).

4 Roll out the rest of the pastry and top the pie. Add decorations out of the leftover pastry, if you like. Bake for 30 minutes, until golden.

ONION OR APPLE?
Peel a large onion and take a great big whiff. Quickly take a bite of an apple. Because our sense of smell and taste are closely linked, the apple will taste like an onion!

How does it work?
When we taste cooked apple, we're tasting a particular combination of molecules.

The ingredients in your cracker pie create a similar mix of molecules to those in apple pie. Could any of your friends tell the difference?

Make a board game

If you've had enough of Monopoly, Cluedo, and Snakes and Ladders, then perhaps it's time to **INVENT YOUR OWN GAME**. You don't need lots of equipment – just pens, card, dice, and, most importantly, people to play with.

Start

The first thing you need to think of is what your game is going to be about (a theme). It can be anything you like!

Can't think of a theme for your game? How about an alien invasion?

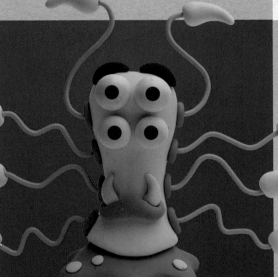

To make the board, divide a sheet of card into squares with a ruler. Decorate the board with drawings that match your theme.

In sequence fill the squares with numbers, from 1 to whatever the final square is.

Make counters out of card. Again, try to make them match your theme.

As a treat, give the winner a bar of chocolate!

GO BACK 3 SPACES

Give your game a trial run to make sure it worksssss

Fill the squares with rules such as "go forward two squares", or "miss a go". It's your game, so make up unusual rules.

MISS A TURN

Roll the dice. The winner is the first person to get to the final square!

Game over

 # Become a detective

Nobody has the same **FINGERPRINTS** as you – they are unique. This makes fingerprints incredibly useful for solving crimes. So, see if you can detect which of your friends has touched what.

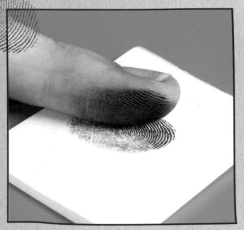

1 Ask your "suspects" to put their fingers on the inkpad then press them into a notebook or paper. Note down whose prints are whose.

2 Send your friends into the kitchen and ask them each to touch just one thing. Now, seek out prints on doors, windows, and mugs.

3 Dip a paintbrush in the cocoa powder, shake off the excess, and apply powder to surfaces that you think might have prints on.

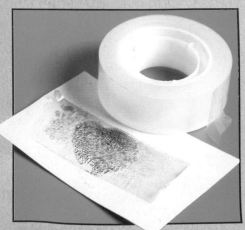

4 When you find a good print, apply a piece of tape and pull it off in one smooth motion. Stick it to a piece of card to preserve it.

5 Compare these prints with those you took earlier. Do you have some matching ones? Can you tell who touched what?

TOP TIP
Afterwards, make sure you clean up and wash your hands. Time for a mug of cocoa and detective movie?

The ridges on your fingertips help you feel the texture of a surface

FINGERPRINT TYPES

There are four main types of fingerprints: loops, whorls, arches, and combination prints. Loops are the most common, and arches are the rarest.

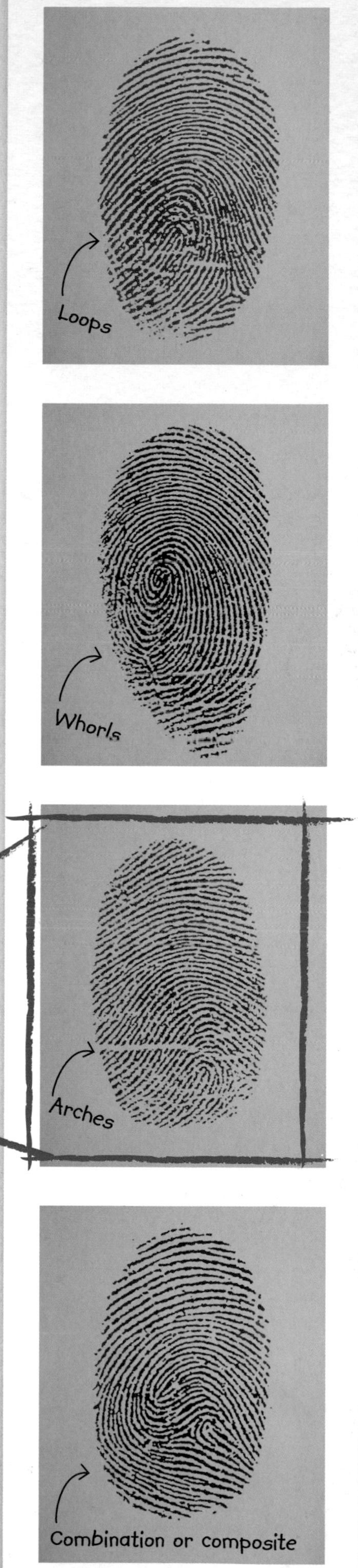

Loops

Whorls

Arches

Combination or composite

You leave prints behind because of the oils on your skin

Magic tricks

Everybody should have a few tricks up their sleeve. If you want to become **A MASTER OF ILLUSION**, then start off with these two simple tricks.

You will need
- One small and two large coins
- Deck of cards

Watch one coin become two

Convince your audience that you've transformed one coin into two before their very eyes, using a sleight of hand. If only!

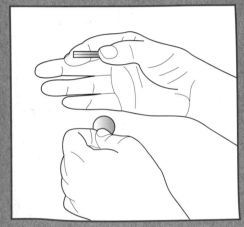

1 Place the two identical coins horizontally between your thumb and index finger. Hold the other coin in your other hand.

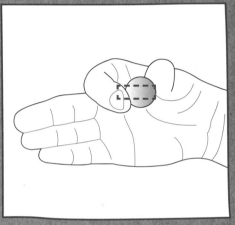

2 Place the smaller coin vertically between your thumb and index finger so it covers the large coins. This is the trick's starting point.

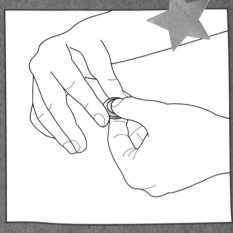

3 Show the small coin to the audience. Put your hands together and use your thumb to slide the smaller coin over the larger ones.

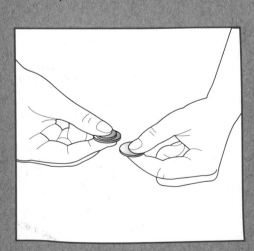

4 Quickly split the coins so that you hold a large coin in one hand, and a large coin with the small coin on top of it in the other hand.

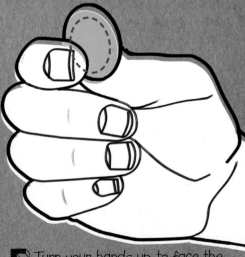

5 Turn your hands up to face the audience. Because the small coin was on top, it will be hidden, leaving just the large coins visible.

Perform the trick quickly so your audience never sees the hidden coin

Card psychic

Fool your friends into thinking they have any say in the matter of this card trick. With a little misdirection, you'll be in charge from *step 1*.

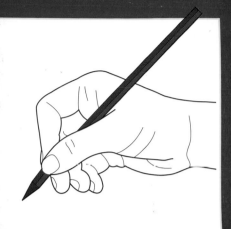

1 Before you start, pick a card, such as the ace of hearts, and put it on top of the deck. Write it on a piece of paper and put it in your pocket.

2 Take the cards and push with your thumb the top four cards into your palm; the ace will be at the bottom. Hold the cards apart with a finger.

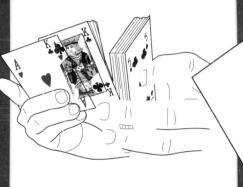

3 Spread the other cards on top and ask someone to point to one. Split the deck at this point, and slide the four hidden cards underneath.

4 Put the deck back together and reveal the *bottom* card to the audience. It'll be the card you put there, not the one pointed to.

5 Reach into your pocket and pull out the piece of paper. Show it to the audience – they'll think you have psychic powers!

Ace of hearts

MISDIRECTION
The secret to a good magic show is being confident and putting on a good show. If you're entertaining in your delivery, you can distract or misdirect the audience to pull off your trick.

If you want to be a **BALLOON WIZARD** then it's good to know that all that twisting and bending is **EASIER THAN IT LOOKS**. So, buy some special balloons and practise making these two simple ones to start with.

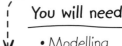

Make a Sword

Be sure to use modelling balloons

You can twist in either direction

1 Blow up a balloon, leaving about 2.5cm (1in) at the end deflated. This extra air stops the balloon from bursting whenever you twist it.

2 Twist the balloon about 12cm (5in) from the knot. Twist it around a few times so that it doesn't unwind when you let go.

Bend about 7.5cm (3in) from the twist, then fold it into the first twist, making a loop

3 Bend the balloon towards the deflated end.

4 Another 7.5cm (3in) from the loop you just made, fold the balloon over and twist it in the same place to make a second loop.

5 Adjust the sword so that it's nice and straight, with the hilt in line with the blade. Time for a wibbly wobbly sword fight!

Grrr, take that!

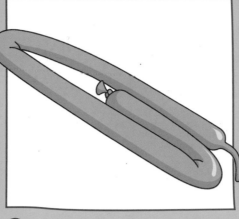

1 Inflate a balloon with about 10cm (4in) deflated. Make a fold about 20cm (8in) away from the Knot.

2 Fold the tail again so that the end lines up with the first fold. The balloon should look a bit like a paperclip.

3 Where all three bits meet – by the Knot – twist together. You should have two loops and a tube sticking up, as shown.

Create a swan

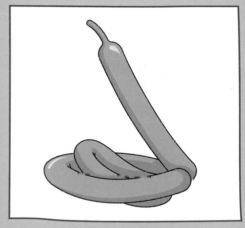

4 Pull one of the loops up through the other one to make the body. The long tube will be the neck and head.

5 Fold the neck down away from the body as shown. Hold the neck tightly, bend, and squeeze it. Let go and it should stay in place.

Balloon dog

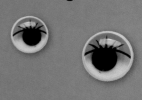

Once your **BALLOON-TASTIC SKILLS** are honed and you're happy bending and twisting (*see pages 68–69*), you'll be ready to tackle this **SLIGHTLY TRICKY DOG**. Well, for now it's a dog but it could easily become a giraffe or who knows what.

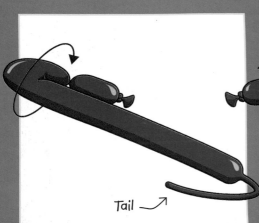

Tail →

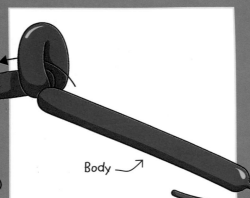

Body →

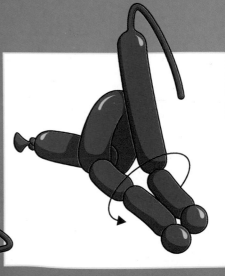

1 Inflate a balloon, leaving an 18cm (7in) tail. Make a bubble about 5cm (2in) for the head, and then make a fold 5cm (2in) away.

2 Make a fold where the body meets the twist, creating a loop, and then push the head (the bubble with the knot) through it.

3 Leave a gap, and then make a 7cm (3in) bubble, two 2.5cm (1in) bubbles, and a 7cm (3in) bubble. Twist the last into the first.

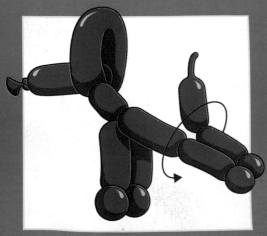

4 Leave a gap about 7cm (3in) long for the body, and then do what you did in step 3 again to make the dog's hind legs.

5 Twist everything into position, and then squeeze the tail a bit, so that some of the air forms a bubble at the back.

Fido

Juggling

Anybody can juggle, you just have to learn how (and put in some practice). Start off with **ONE BALL, THEN TWO**, and you'll soon have **THREE BALLS** in the air, or even more...

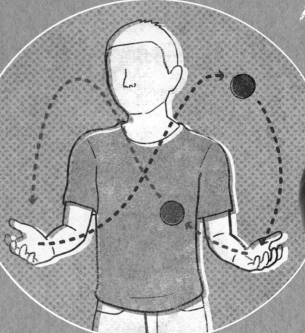

2 Once you can do this every time without looking, add a second ball. When the first ball is at its highest peak, throw the second one just below it with the same looping motion.

Start here

1 Start off with one ball. Toss it in a looping motion from one hand to the other, starting off low. Try to get it to peak at the same height every time. Now, practise.

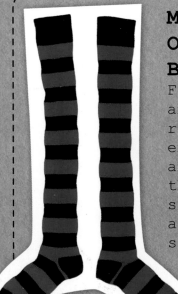

MAKE YOUR OWN JUGGLING BALLS
Fill the end of an old sock with rice. Tie the end tightly and cut off the excess sock with a pair of scissors.

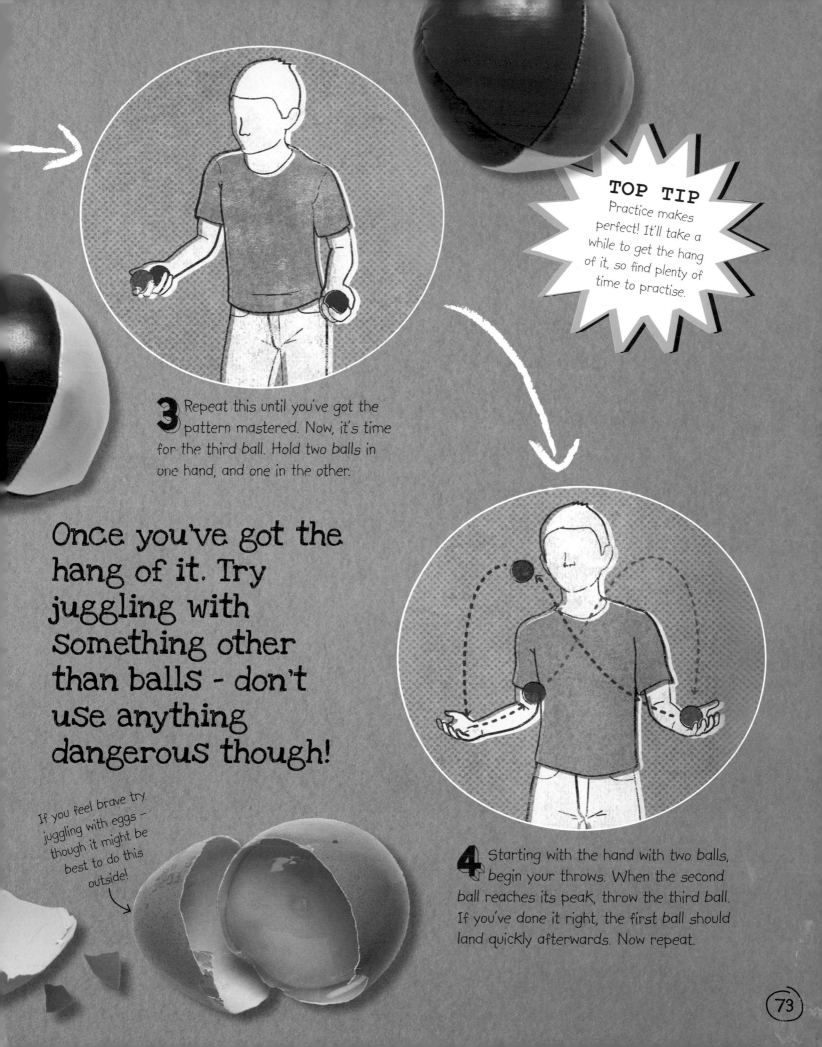

TOP TIP
Practice makes perfect! It'll take a while to get the hang of it, so find plenty of time to practise.

3 Repeat this until you've got the pattern mastered. Now, it's time for the third ball. Hold two balls in one hand, and one in the other.

Once you've got the hang of it. Try juggling with Something other than balls - don't use anything dangerous though!

If you feel brave try juggling with eggs – though it might be best to do this outside!

4 Starting with the hand with two balls, begin your throws. When the second ball reaches its peak, throw the third ball. If you've done it right, the first ball should land quickly afterwards. Now repeat.

Want to be the next **JAMES BOND**? Collect great **GADGETS**? Be a master of **DISGUISE**? Here's the basics you'll need for any **SPY IN TRAINING**.

A NEWSPAPER PROP

When you're shadowing a target you sometimes need to hide in plain sight. By cutting some eyeholes out of a newspaper you can watch your target without them seeing you.

DISGUISES

When a spy's cover is blown his mission is usually over. That's why a spy has to become a master of disguise. Experiment with ways to slip by undetected or to create new aliases. Here are some suggestions:

> Hats
> Moustaches
> Glasses
> Wigs

BLENDING IN

A disguise should help you blend in, not stand out. So anything that looks over the top will only make you look suspicious!

TOP TIP
For more spy gear, don't forget the periscope (pages 10–11) and secret book safe (pages 20–21.)

Invisible ink

Relay a secret message to a friend using this invisible ink. We use a picture to give you the general idea.

1 Put equal parts of baking soda and water into a bowl and stir together. You don't need much, and the baking soda won't fully dissolve, but that doesn't matter.

2 Dip the cotton bud into the mixture and use it to write on the paper. Let the paper dry and slip it to your accomplice (look out for people over your shoulder).

3 The reader has to hold a hairdryer near to the paper to reveal the hidden message!

The heat of the hairdryer reacts with the baking soda and spells out your message

Prank patrol

If you're looking for a fun way to mess with your friends or family, why not pull a **PRACTICAL JOKE**? Remember though, if you're going to become a prankster, you have to be ready when people want to get **THEIR OWN BACK**!

A Surprise Soaking

1 Fill a plastic bottle with water and tighten the lid. Write "DO NOT OPEN" on the label and put it outdoors where someone will see it.

2 Carefully poke a few small holes in the side of the bottle with a pin. If the lid is tight enough, none of the water should come out.

3 Curiosity will eventually get the better of anyone who sees it and they will open the bottle. When they do the water will spray out of the holes and soak them!

HOW IT WORKS

This trick works because of AIR PRESSURE. When the bottle's lid is on, the air pressure outside the bottle stops water from leaking out. When you take the lid off, air can rush into the bottle, which pushes on the water and forces it out through the holes.

Soap trick
Take a bar of soap and cover it in with clear nail varnish. Let it dry properly and then put it back. The nail varnish will stop the soap from lathering, and nobody will know why!

Flyswatter gross out
You'll need an accomplice for this trick. Ask an adult to buy you a brand new flyswatter. (Whatever you do, don't use an old one!) Squash a few raisins into it and find a person to prank. Show them the flyswatter and say "watch this". Then lick the raisins off the swatter and laugh at the horrified look on their face as they think you're eating flies!

Moving coin
Tape a length of dental floss to a coin and leave it in a public place. Hide out of sight and when someone bends down to pick up the coin, pull it away at the last second.

SWEET NOT SALTY
Get one over on your family by switching the salt in the saltshaker with sugar. Try not to laugh when everyone wonders why their food tastes strange!

Spot the difference

Do you have a good **EYE FOR DETAIL**? Look at the pictures on each page. They may look the same at first glance, but there are six differences between them. Can you spot them all?

Answers:

6. The jelly has a different number of lumps

1. The frogs are a different shade of green and the other is purple   2. One of the little blue squares is upside down   3. One of the robots is blue   4. The gingerbread man has a different number of buttons   5. The Knight is missing his eye

 # Flipbook animation

Bring your **DRAWINGS TO LIFE**. A flipbook animation is a series of pictures that change a little bit each time, so that it **LOOKS LIKE IT MOVES** if you flick through them! Tell a little cartoon story, such as a fish eating another fish.

1 Decide on what you want to animate. It can *be* anything you want, but keep it simple at first. Start on the *back* page and lightly sketch your first drawing.

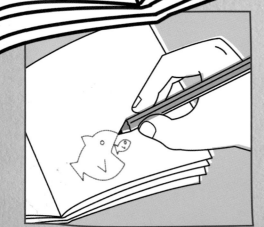

2 Working *backwards*, sketch the other stages. It might seem strange, but it means that you can trace parts that look the same.

3 Every few pages, flip the pages to check that your animation looks okay. Fix any problems with your eraser.

4 When you're happy with it, go over the lines in *bold* and add colour. Thumb through the pages and see the animation in all its glory!

Have a doodle
to come up
with ideas!

STOP MOTION

Your animation can be based on photos too. For example, take a photograph of a glass of water. Take a sip without moving it, then take another photo, and repeat. Combine the pictures using software on a computer. You'll see the water vanish.

ANIMATION IDEAS

If you can't think of what to draw, copy the sequence below. Once you've got the hang of it, you can try a bouncing ball or a moving stick man. It's up to you!

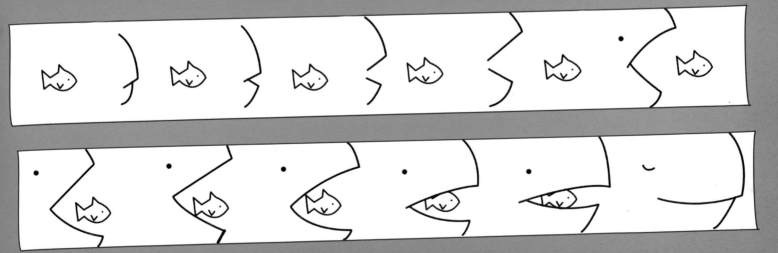

Write a Scary Story

There's no need to save all the scaring for Halloween. Whether you want to amass your own set of scary stories or invite friends over for a **SCARY STORYTELLING SESSION**, here's the basics for any young writer in training.

PICK A THEME

The best writers draw ideas from real life. Try to think of what scares you and make it a part of your story. Whether it's ghosts, aliens, monsters, or something else – it'll be easier for you to imagine what your characters will feel like if you think like they would!

Structure

Every good story needs a beginning, middle, and an end.

Don't concentrate on anything specific at this point, it's just to help you later.

Before you start, sketch up a quick outline or map of how your story might end and begin, and then think of ways to connect the two.

BUILD TENSION

Suspense – or not knowing what's going to happen – is what makes a story scary. Try to keep the audience on their toes by not making it obvious what's going to happen next.

SCENE SETTING

To make your story believable, it needs to feel like it takes place somewhere real. It all depends on what your theme is. If you really want to make your story scary, have it take place somewhere your friends know, that will make it easier for them to imagine it being real!

Hero

Your story needs a character for people to identify with. It's up to you what kind of person they can be: male, female, strong, weak, scared, fearless. Sometimes the best characters are flawed. Think of what your character would be thinking or feeling and work it into the story.

Villain

Every story needs a convincing villain, and the best ones are the ones that are equal but opposite to the hero. They can be supernatural, a person, a monster – it's up to you. Just be sure to focus on the villain as much as the hero.

AND TO FINISH

The ending is usually what the audience will remember most, so make it memorable. You can have a happy ending, a funny one to break the tension, or a "twist", where something totally unexpected happens. The most important part of the ending is always to leave the reader wanting more. Time for a sequel?

83

Unusual ball games

If you've had your fill of football, tennis, basketball, cricket, or rugby, but want to **MESS ABOUT WITH A BALL**, then here are a few unusual games that you might have never heard of.

DOWN ON ONE KNEE

Everyone stands in a circle, throwing a tennis ball to each other. Every time someone drops a catchable throw, they "lose a limb" – for the first time they go down on one knee, then both knees, then have one arm behind their back. Miss four in a row and you're out, but for every successful catch you get one limb back. So, don't give up!

DODGE IT!

Everybody starts with five points and spreads out. Choose one player to be "it" first. The player who is "it" throws a large, soft ball at one of the other players. This player can either **CATCH THE BALL** or **DODGE IT**. If they're hit, they lose a point, but if they catch it, the player who threw it loses a point. If the ball lands on the floor, anybody can pick it up and become **"IT"**. When a player loses five points, they're out of the game. The last player left is the winner.

Use a soft ball for this game!

CATCH-EGORIES

Choose a category, such as animals, and get everybody to stand in a circle. Take turns naming players and throwing them the ball. That player has to say the name of an animal before catching the ball. If you're too slow, repeat, or drop the ball, you're out!

BALL RELAY

Mix up a simple race to include balls somehow. Walk with a ball between your legs, dribble a basketball around, or pass a football between each other as you run to the finish line.

Use a large ball so it isn't too hard to catch

Let's have a water fight!

When the temperature's rising what could be better than a team game mixed with a **WATER FIGHT**? This game – **CAPTURE THE FLAG** – requires speed, accuracy, teamwork, and tactics. So, who will **WIN** and who will get the **WETTEST**?

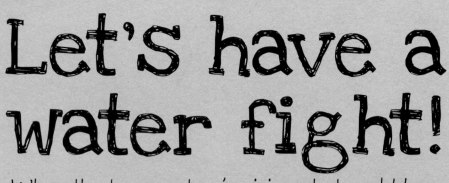

How to play

Fill up water balloons and split into two teams. Place a different coloured flag at two bases at opposite ends of a field or park.

The object of the game is to capture the other team's flag and take it back to your base. In order to score, **BOTH** flags have to be at your base.

TACTIC #1

Teamwork is important. Each team needs a captain, who'll then give each player a job to do – attack or defence. If everybody tried to capture the flag, there wouldn't be anybody left to defend their own!

RULES

- **WATER BALLOONS ONLY,** water guns are too easy to hit people with!

- If you get hit, you have to leave the field for a **30-SECOND TIME-OUT** before you are allowed to re-enter the game.

- If you're hit while carrying a flag, drop it on the floor where you are. Either team can then pick it up to capture it or return it to base.

- The first team to **THREE CAPTURES** wins.

TACTIC #3

Try to coordinate attacks to knock out several of the other team at once, so they're on time-out at the same time. Then there won't be many left to defend their base and flag.

TACTIC #2

Pay attention to ammo supplies. Don't waste your ammo on long throws, try to get in close. Also, check out the other team's ammo levels – when they're low that's the perfect time to attack!

During the festival of Songkran, people all over Thailand have a giant water fight in the streets!

Outdoor games

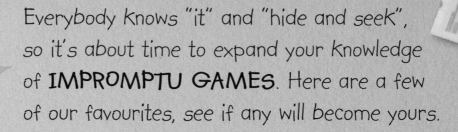

Everybody knows "it" and "hide and seek", so it's about time to expand your knowledge of **IMPROMPTU GAMES**. Here are a few of our favourites, see if any will become yours.

Red light, green light

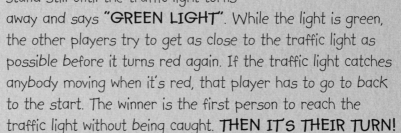

One player is chosen to be a **TRAFFIC LIGHT,** and stands by a tree while everybody else stands way back. When the traffic light faces the other players, they all have to stand still until the traffic light turns away and says **"GREEN LIGHT"**. While the light is green, the other players try to get as close to the traffic light as possible before it turns red again. If the traffic light catches anybody moving when it's red, that player has to go to back to the start. The winner is the first person to reach the traffic light without being caught. **THEN IT'S THEIR TURN!**

A human chain

Two players are chosen to be "it" and hold hands. Their job is to catch the other players. Whenever they catch someone, that person joins the chain by linking hands, and they have to try to catch everybody else.

Freeze it

If you can play "it" then "freeze it" is a great variation. Instead of becoming "it" when you are caught, you have to remain frozen in place until another player unfreezes you by tapping you on the shoulder. Will you be a hero, or try to survive on your own?

Off the ground

Inflate a balloon and get everyone to stand in a big circle. Someone starts by batting the balloon high into the air and nominating another player. That player has to get to the balloon before it hits the ground and knock it back up, saying the next player's name. If a player doesn't stop the balloon from hitting the ground on their turn, they sit out until the game is over. The winner is the last person left!

Hot footing around

Lay down sheets of newspaper a few metres apart to build a chain of "islands". Players have to get around the course as fast as possible, jumping from island to island without touching the "sea" between.

Players can choose to remain as one long chain, or split into smaller chains to round up the other players, as long as they are connected to at least one person. The last person to be caught is the winner.

Making camp

There's nothing quite like **SLEEPING UNDER THE STARS**. But it's not always practical to go camp in a woodland or by a stream. But don't let that stop you; there's always the garden or even the living room. Plus, at home there's the benefit of unlimited hot chocolate!

You will need

- Tents
- Ground sheets
- Air mattresses
- Sleeping bags
- Pillows
- Torches

Setting up

Make like pioneers of the **WILD WEST** and set up your camp before it gets dark. Put the tents in a big circle, with a space in the middle for everyone to gather round. Ask adults to help you put the tents up, lay down ground sheets, and pump up air mattresses so you've got a comfy place to wriggle into your sleeping bag. A picnic table and chairs go perfectly in the middle.

Indoor camps

If you don't have a tent you can build a makeshift one from blankets and chairs! The bigger the better.

Games

The best part of camping is being **OUTDOORS** with your **FRIENDS**, when you're **FREE TO DO MUCH MORE** than you could in the house. So, who's up for some "caterpillar races" (in sleeping bags), "blanket tug of war", or freeze tag?

Campfire grub

Cooking over **A FIRE** is one of the joys of camping, but having a fire in your back garden isn't necessarily a good idea! Luckily, the **KITCHEN IS NEARBY** so you can prepare your food and bring it out on trays. Or, if you're camping with adults, ask them to set up the **BBQ**. What is **YOUR FAVOURITE CAMPING FOOD?**

Hot dogs

Toasted marshmallows

Does anybody know any good campfire stories?

Cookies

Beans

Burgers

91

Playing pirates

AHOY THERE! Pirates live a life of adventure on the high seas, and so can you! Search for the **BURIED TREASURE** and **DO BATTLE** against your fellow pirates with these fab props.

You will need

- Two pieces of cardboard
- Glue
- Black tape
- Tin foil

Cardboard cutlass

The cutlass is the weapon of choice of pirates everywhere. So if you plan on sailing the seven seas, you'll need one of your own.

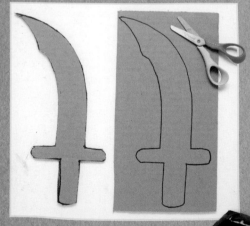

1 Mark out the cutlass shape on two pieces of cardboard as shown. Cut them out and glue them together.

2 Once the glue has dried, wrap black tape around the hilt, and foil around the blade.

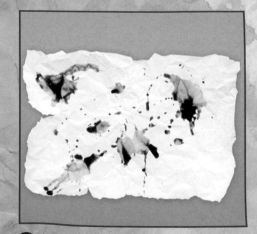

Treasure map

Any pirate worth his salt is always looking to bag some booty. Here's a fun way of making your own treasure map. If you want, you can make a map of your house or garden and hide something for your friends to find.

1 Tear around the edges of a piece of paper. Crumple it into a ball, then flatten it out, and lie it on old newspaper or card.

2 Put a few spoonfuls of the tea or coffee onto the paper and rub it in with your hands. Try to cover the whole page.

3 Wait for five minutes and get an adult to dry it with the hairdryer. Make sure that they don't hold the hairdryer too close to the page.

4 Once it's dried and looks old, use the markers to draw landmarks on your map. Show rocks, jungles, caves, and don't forget X marks the spot!

Olympics outdoors

The **OLYMPIC GAMES** may only come around every four years, but if you host your own, you can go for gold whenever you want!

INVITE YOUR FRIENDS over and make a list of events you want to compete in. It's up to you to decide which ones, but try to have at least five. Here are a few suggestions:

Bean bag shot putt

Obstacle Course

Standing long jump

Hoop toss

Relay race

Three-legged race

Flying discus

MAKING MEDALS

You can't have an Olympics without medals. Before you start, work out how many events you're going to have, and make three medals (gold, silver, and bronze) for each one.

Egg and spoon race

Bin basketball

Sack race

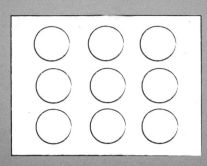

1 Use the can as a guide on the card to draw around to make circles. Draw enough for all your upcoming Olympic events.

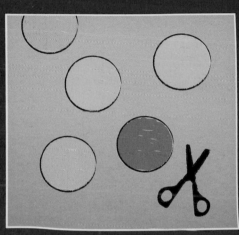

2 Cut the circles out and either paint or colour them in with markers. Make one-third of them gold or yellow, one-third silver or grey, and the last third brown.

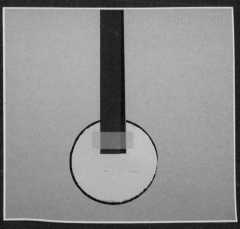

3 Cut the ribbon into lengths that are long enough to hang around your neck. Tape them to the back of the card to finish the medals.

3   1   2   ON THE PODIUM

Once the events are over, award the winners their medals on a podium. Make one from anything strong enough to support your weight, such as crates or wooden boxes.

Throw a party

EVERYBODY LOVES a party. Rather than go with the usual party games, why not try some of these out to make your next party a MEMORABLE one.

Party games

When thinking about what games to play, there are, of course, the PARTY CLASSICS – pass-the-parcel, Simon says, and musical chairs. But you can mix them up with something NEW. If your party has a theme, invent or adapt games to match it.

Or, pick one of these four...

Invitations

Not only do invitations tell your guests when and where the party is, but also if there are any special requirements. So if it's a FANCY DRESS party or guests need to BRING SOMETHING along, include that info too.

You can buy invitations, but WHY NOT TRY TO MAKE YOUR OWN that are more personal? That way, if your party has a theme, you can make invitations that match.

Key stalker

A set of keys are placed under a chair in the middle of a room. One player is blindfolded and sits on the chair, while everybody else stands in a circle around them. EVERYBODY TAKES TURNS TO TRY TO SNEAK UP AND STEAL THE KEYS WITHOUT THE BLINDFOLDED PLAYER NOTICING. If the blindfolded player thinks they have detected someone, they have to point at the player and say

"I see you!"

If a player manages to steal the keys and take them back to the circle without being caught, it's their turn to be blindfolded.

TOP TIP

Use a set of keys with a lot of keyrings. The noisier they are, the harder it will be to steal them!

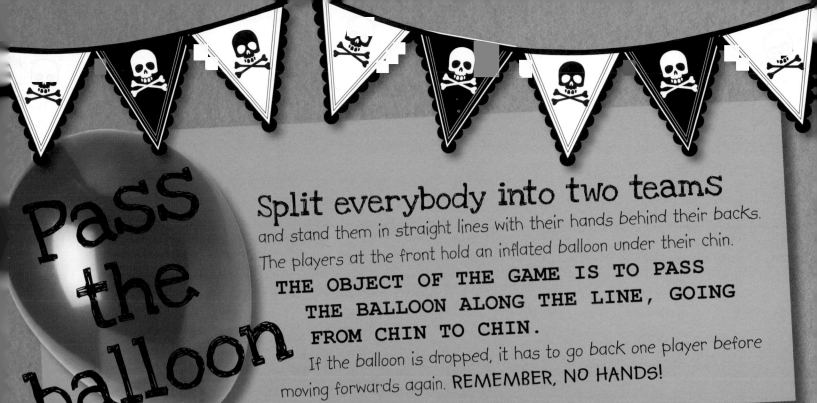

Pass the balloon

Split everybody into two teams and stand them in straight lines with their hands behind their backs. The players at the front hold an inflated balloon under their chin. **THE OBJECT OF THE GAME IS TO PASS THE BALLOON ALONG THE LINE, GOING FROM CHIN TO CHIN.** If the balloon is dropped, it has to go back one player before moving forwards again. **REMEMBER, NO HANDS!**

Musical statues

Choose one person to be **THE JUDGE**. It's their job to stand with their back to everybody and play music while everybody dances. After a few seconds the judge **PAUSES THE MUSIC AND TURNS AROUND.** The other players have to freeze, like statues! **ANYBODY CAUGHT MOVING IS OUT.**

The memory game

Place 10–15 small objects from around the house on a tray. Sit everyone in a circle and put the tray in the middle. Players get a minute to memorize as many objects as possible. **ONCE THE TIME IS UP, HIDE THE TRAY AND GIVE OUT PENS AND PAPER.** They have two minutes to write down as many objects as they can remember. **WHOEVER WRITES DOWN THE MOST OBJECTS IS THE WINNER.**

TOP TIP
Pick objects that are different shapes, sizes, and colours – some strange, some ordinary.

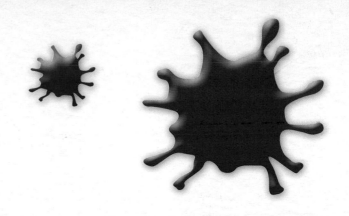

Know it

Impress your friends by throwing **AMAZING FACTS AND TRIVIA** about all sorts of things – from dinosaurs to robots – into your conversations. And to top that, show off your **NEW-FOUND SKILLS** as a **SPORTS PRO**, and a **LIFE-SAVING HERO** when out and about. What's not to like?

✓ A world of robots

Sci-fi films like to portray robots in a dramatic role taking over **A FUTURISTIC WORLD**. But, robots are already **HERE** and are **WORKING TIRELESSLY** for us – making cars, exploring the world, and even operating on people.

ROBOTS IN SPACE

Because of the harsh conditions of outer space, NASA now uses robots in many of their missions. In 2012, the Curiosity rover was transported millions of miles away to explore the surface of Mars.

nautile
lfremer
nautile
lfremer nautile

ALL-TERRAIN VEHICLES

Robots make the **BEST EXPLORERS**, because they can go places that humans can't. They have been everywhere – from the **BOTTOM OF THE OCEAN** to **OUTER SPACE**.

FACTORY ROBOTS

Most of the world's robots work in factories. They are perfect for such work because they can do precise tasks for a long time — and never get tired!

The first working robots date back to the 1960s

The word "robot" comes from the **CZECH WORD "ROBOTA"**, which means forced labour

Did you know?

In 2012, there are about **10 MILLION** robots around the world, most of them are found working in factories.

Robots are also used for **RESEARCH**, at universities, and by the **ARMY**.

There is even a robot called **"DA VINCI"** that performs **OPERATIONS** in more than 1,500 hospitals around the world.

Prehistoric trivia

It's been **65 MILLION YEARS** since dinosaurs walked the Earth, but we're still discovering **NEW INFORMATION** about these amazing creatures. How many of these facts do you know?

On the land

The word dinosaur means **TERRIBLE LIZARD**, but they weren't all that terrible! After all, they ruled the Earth for almost 165 million years! Here are a few things you may not know about them:

SUE, the *Tyrannosaurus Rex* fossil at the Field Museum, Chicago, USA is the most complete *T Rex* fossil in the world, and cost the museum **£5.2 MILLION ($8.4 MILLION!)** in 1997CE.

Because different dinosaurs existed in different time periods, less time separates us from the *Tyrannosaurus Rex* than separated the *T Rex* from the *Stegosaurus*, for example!

One of the **SMALLEST** dinosaurs, the *Compsognathus*, could run at **INCREDIBLE SPEEDS** of almost 40mph (64kph).

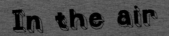

In the air

DINOSAURS COULDN'T FLY, but at the same time as dinosaurs walked the earth, their reptile relatives PTEROSAURS SOARED IN THE SKIES.

The largest creature ever to fly was the pterosaur Quezalcoatlus. Its wingspan alone was 12M (40FT) – almost the size of A SMALL AEROPLANE.

Pterosaurs had THIN HOLLOW BONES, which made it much easier to fly.

Today's modern BIRDS are actually the closest living relatives to dinosaurs!

In the sea

While dinosaurs ruled the land, MARINE REPTILES ruled the sea. Although they seem similar, and became extinct at the same time, they were actually COMPLETELY UNRELATED TO DINOSAURS.

The skull of Deinosuchus – a relative of modern crocodiles – was 1.8m (6ft) long, and a fully grown Deinosuchus weighed up to 5 TONNES.

Because they lived in the sea, where fossilization is more likely, there are lots of well-preserved fossils of marine reptiles today.

The ancestor of the Great White Shark, the Megalodon, are thought to have been up to 20M (65FT) LONG!

Musical experiments

Even celebrated musicians were beginners once, so take heart that with **SOME PRACTICE** you too can **LEARN TO PLAY** an instrument. Here is a basic guide to playing a few guitar chords and an actual tune on the piano.

Who knows, you could be **WELL ON YOUR WAY** to a hit song.

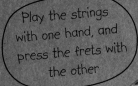

Play the strings with one hand, and press the frets with the other

Guitar basics

If you strum across a guitar's strings while you press by a **FRET**, you'll make a note. When you play certain combinations of strings and frets together, it's called a **CHORD**.

Fret

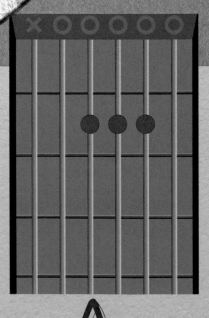

CHORDS
A lot of songs are made up of just these four chords. Press your fingers on the strings (see spots, as shown) and strum all the strings. Give each one a try.

A

Playing the piano

Each piano key has its own note, so anybody can play a tune – all you have to do is press the keys! The hard part is doing it in a sequence that makes a nice melody.

KEEP PRACTISING!

"HAPPY BIRTHDAY TO YOU..."
Impress your friends by playing the sequence of notes below in the rhythm of this famous tune.

G   G   A   G   C   B
G   G   A   G   C   B
G   G   G   E   D   B
F   F   E   C   B   A
          E   C   C
             D

Black keys are sharp and flat notes

Middle C

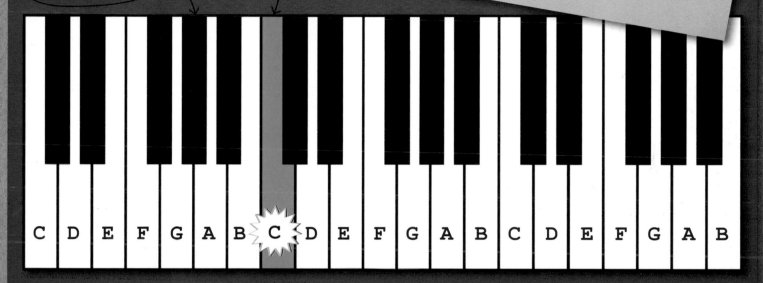

C D E F G A B C D E F G A B C D E F G A B C D E F G A B

Don't play the strings with an X

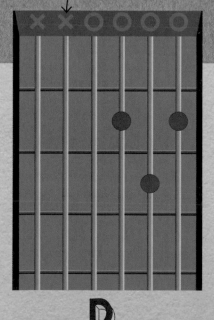

D

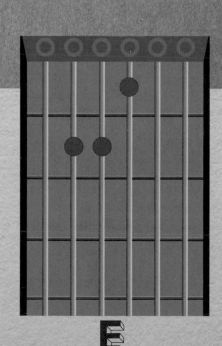

E

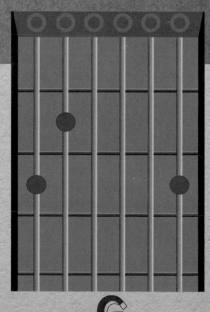

G

Castles and forts

Did you know that a castle is **DIFFERENT** from a fort? Well, you soon will with our lowdown on essential **FACTS** of these buildings of bygone eras.

What's the difference?

Although they might seem similar, castles and forts aren't the same thing.

A **CASTLE** is a building – often where an important person or leader lives – that is built to withstand an attack by enemies.

A **FORT** or fortress on the other hand, is used only by the military and houses troops at certain strategic locations.

Chateau de Bonaquil Fortress, Aquitaine, France

Keep out!

The main purpose of a castle is to **KEEP ATTACKERS OUT**. Gates could only be opened from inside, and were surrounded by thick, tall walls that were hard to breach or climb. Towers were built with small holes in the side, so that archers could **FIRE ON** attackers without being exposed. Even the staircases were built with defence in mind – they were built in a narrow spiral so attackers had to come up one by one.

Why not try building a cardboard castle

Natural defence

The location of a castle or fort could be its best defence. Castles were typically built **AT THE TOP OF HILLS** – not only did this make it easier to see approaching troops, but it made it harder for a successful enemy attack.

They were also often built **NEAR WATER**. As well as offering an extra layer of defence (a moat, for instance), having an on-site water supply is handy when under siege!

Marksburg Castle, Braubach, Germany

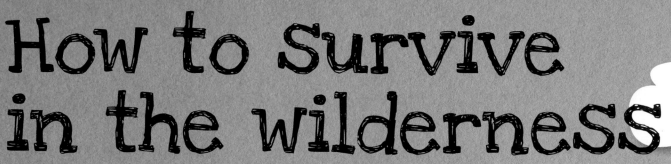

How to Survive in the wilderness

Follow in the footsteps of the great adventurers by having a few **SURVIVAL SKILLS** up your sleeve. Learn how to keep on **THE RIGHT TRACK** and know what to do if you do **GET LOST**.

Try to imagine what the landscape will look like from the air while you walk through it. This **MENTAL PICTURE** will help you see the route you've taken.

When you're exploring, be alert to the terrain all around you, not just what lies ahead. Occasionally, check **BEHIND YOU** so that you can see where you've come from, just in case you need to retrace your steps.

LANDMARKS, such as a memorable tree or a **WEIRD-LOOKING ROCK**, can help you navigate and remind you of your route, so keep an eye out for those. Streams and rivers can also help you work out where you are.

If you do get lost...

The last thing you want to do is get even more lost and become exhausted. So recognize that you're lost and try to find north.

Finding north

If you ever need to get your bearings, being able to find which way is north is really useful and you'll be able to work out which direction you need to head in. So, if you forgot to pack a compass, try out these DIY versions. Remember the order of the points by thinking **N**ever **E**at **S**limy **W**orms, clockwise.

Shadow Compass

1 Push a stick into the ground and look for its shadow. Mark the end of the shadow with a stone and mark it with a W, for west.

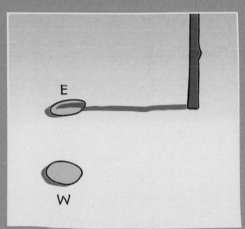

2 Wait 30 minutes. As the Sun has moved west, the stick's shadow will have moved east. Mark this point with an E, for east.

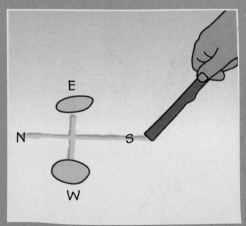

3 Draw a line *between* east and west, then draw another line at right angles to it for north and south. Mark N and S to finish..

watch compass

LOST NORTH OF THE EQUATOR?

Take off your watch and hold it flat, so that the hour hand points to the Sun. Find the point halfway between the hour hand and 12 o'clock. This halfway point will be pointing south, so the opposite way is north.

LOST SOUTH OF THE EQUATOR?

Position your watch so that the 12 o'clock mark points to the Sun. Find the halfway point between the 12 o'clock mark and the hour hand. This will be north.

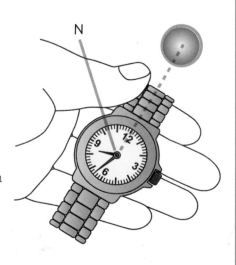

Spotting deadly snakes

Snakes aren't as dangerous as you might think. Most, in fact, **AREN'T VENOMOUS AT ALL**, and the ones that are usually bite only in self-defence. Most of the snakes here all have **POISONOUS VENOM**. Find out more about these killer reptiles and **WHERE IN THE WORLD THEY LIVE**.

Gaboon viper
This African hunter has the **LARGEST FANGS** of any venomous snake. It is also a master of camouflage, stalking its prey while hidden among leaves.

King cobra
The King cobra, found in the forests of India and Southeast Asia, is the **WORLD'S LONGEST** venomous snake – growing to be up to 5m (16ft) long.

Hognosed pit viper

This **ENDANGERED SPECIES** of snake is found in Mexico and South America. Adult males are **PRETTY SMALL**, in snake terms, and grow to be only 40cm (16in) long.

Rattlesnake

Found in the Americas, rattlesnakes live in hot, dry places. They **SHAKE THE LOOSE SCALES** at the end of their tails to threaten their enemies, but it's their bite that makes them dangerous.

MORE THAN A BITE

It's not just fangs that can be deadly. Some snakes, such as the **BOA CONSTRICTOR**, use their strong bodies to wrap around their prey and literally squeeze the air out of them.

Mangrove

Sometimes called "Boiga", this species of snake can be found in Asia, India, and Australia. They vary in pattern and colour, but have **DISTINCTLY LARGE HEADS AND EYES**.

ultimate animal quiz

Do you know your amphibians from your reptiles, and your gorillas from your gibbons? Take our animal quiz to see if you're the real **KING OF THE JUNGLE.**

Ask your friends these questions too. Who can answer the most?

1 All owls have teeth – **TRUE OR FALSE?**

2 The Bengal tiger is found in Africa – **TRUE OR FALSE?**

3 Roughly how many muscles are found in an elephant's trunk?

- 100
- 1,000
- 10,000
- 100,000

4 Bats are the only mammals that have the ability to fly – **TRUE OR FALSE?**

6 A female gorilla was taught to understand more than 2,000 words of English – **TRUE OR FALSE?**

5 The poison dart frog has enough venom to kill 10 adults. On average, how big are they?

- 2.5cm (1in)   • 15cm (6in)   • 20cm (8in)

7 How fast can the deadly great white shark swim?

- 25mph (40kph)
- 35mph (50kph)
- 70mph (110kph)

Cook up a storm

Get ahead of other budding Masterchef contestants by getting to grips with the **RULES OF A KITCHEN** and **HOW TO COOK** your favourite foods without poisoning anyone or cutting off a finger in the process.

Make sure to keep the kitchen clean. Spills can cause accidents!

Safety and hygiene

The Kitchen can be a dangerous place. There are spills, sharp tools, and hot pans to worry about, so safety is very important. Whenever you cook, always bear these things in mind.

Always **WASH YOUR HANDS** before preparing food, as well as any fruit or vegetables.

Always check the use-by dates on your ingredients, and **NEVER COOK FOOD THAT HAS GONE OFF**

Always wear oven gloves when handling hot trays, pans, and tins

Take extra special care when chopping ingredients. **KNIVES NEED TO BE HANDLED VERY CAREFULLY.**

Any Knives or chopping boards used to prepare **RAW MEAT, POULTRY,** or **FISH** should be cleaned properly with hot soapy water before being used again.

Cooks tips

The more prepared you are, the easier cooking is. These simple tips will help keep you out of hot water!

PREPARE your ingredients before you start cooking. That way you can concentrate on what you're doing instead of worrying about it halfway through.

Quantities of ingredients are given in metric or imperial measurements. You can use either, but don't mix the two up

PREHEAT THE OVEN FOR ABOUT 10 MINUTES SO IT'S THE RIGHT TEMPERATURE WHEN YOU PLACE THE FOOD INSIDE

ALWAYS USE THE TYPE OF FLOUR (PLAIN, STRONG, SELF-RAISING) THAT THE RECIPE STATES. It makes all the difference to light sponges and crispy biscuits.

Abbreviations

Recipes can seem confusing at first because of all the abbreviations they contain. Here are the most common ones you'll come across:

Metric:

g = gram
ml = millilitre

Imperial:

oz = ounce
lb = pound
fl oz = fluid ounces

Spoon measures:

tsp = teaspoon
tbsp = tablespoon

 # Play like a pro

Brush up on a few **KEY SKILLS** in football, tennis, and ten-pin bowling and, with a bit of practice, you'll **BLOW THE COMPETITION AWAY** the next time you're playing sport with friends or family.

SCORE A PENALTY

The world's best players rarely miss penalties in practice, but during a game when the pressure is on, things get hard. Here's how to get an edge!

1 Practise taking penalties in an empty goal. Aim for the spots the goalkeeper will have the hardest time reaching: the high and low corners.

2 When you're ready to practise with a goalkeeper. Try to confuse the keeper by looking at different spots, so he can't predict your kick.

3 Kick the ball after a short run up. Don't blast it, as you won't be able to control it – try to place your shot into the corner.

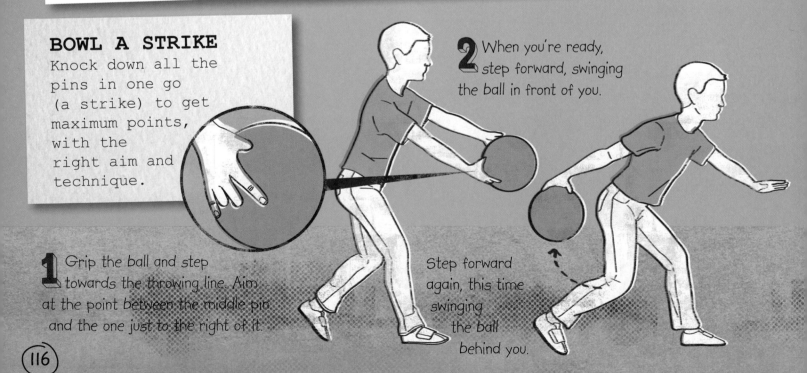

BOWL A STRIKE

Knock down all the pins in one go (a strike) to get maximum points, with the right aim and technique.

2 When you're ready, step forward, swinging the ball in front of you.

1 Grip the ball and step towards the throwing line. Aim at the point between the middle pin and the one just to the right of it.

Step forward again, this time swinging the ball behind you.

HIT A SERVE

A powerful serve is a good way to get an upper hand on your opponent. Practise this shot and you'll soon be hitting aces!

1 Throw the ball into the air in front of you. Bend your left knee and turn your body slightly away from the court.

2 As the ball comes down from its highest point, swing your racket up to hit it. Follow through and get ready for the return!

3 When the ball is high behind you, bend your knees and roll the ball forward in a fluid motion.

Release it and watch all the pins fall!

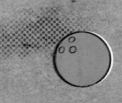

Cowboy capers

Make like a cowboy in the Wild West and learn **HOW TO MAKE AND USE A LASSO**. You might not have herds of cattle to round up or need to lasso and bring down calves to brand, but it **FEELS GREAT** to try – practise on **A CHAIR**. Cowboy hat optional, but yee-haws essential.

Yee-haw Cowboy!

1 After making your lasso, hold the rope coil in one hand. Make a noose 60cm (24in) across, and hold it above the knot, in your other hand.

2 Hold your lasso to the side and spin it around in a clockwise motion. Relax your wrist so that it rotates nice and smoothly.

3 While still rotating the lasso, lift it over your head. Swing the rope as if you were spinning a hoop around your wrist.

Tie a lariat knot

Here's how to tie the special knot – a lariat – to make a lasso work.

Howdy partner!

Tie a knot here to keep the lariat's shape

Feed this end through the loop to finish

1 Make a loose loop in a length of rope. Slip the end of the rope through it.

2 Pull the end of the rope back up through the loop, as shown.

3 Tighten the left loop, leaving a small "eye" in the rope.

4 Pull the knot tight. Then feed the long end of rope through the eye.

TOP TIP
You'll need plenty of room to swing your lasso, so take a chair outside to practise your new cowboy skills.

4 Aim at the chair and bring your hand forward. Let go of the noose. It should shoot forward in front of you.

5 If your aim is spot on, the noose should wrap around the chair. Pull the rope tight to tighten the noose around it. Yee-hah!

That's impossible!

Jaws will be **DROPPING OPEN** in amazement when you show friends and family any of these **UNBELIEVABLE TRICKS**. Afterwards, you can show them how it works or keep it secret.

Egg in a bottle

Ask your friends if they can think of a way to get a boiled egg into a bottle without breaking it. After they've given up trying, show them how it's done.

1 Boil and peel an egg and place it on the rim of the bottle. Show your friends that there's no way the egg will fit through.

2 Ask an adult to light two matches and drop them into the bottle. Quickly place the egg on the rim.

Air presses on the egg from outside

HOW IT WORKS
When the matches go out, the warm air inside the bottle cools and the pressure drops. The air pressure outside the bottle is now higher, so the air tries to push its way in, taking the egg with it.

3 After a few seconds the egg will squeeze through the bottle neck into the bottom of the bottle.

TOP TIP
You might need to try out a few glass bottle shapes to see which fits an egg best.

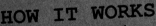

120

Gravity-defying forks

With some precise positioning, you can balance things in ways that seem impossible. It's all about controlling an object's centre of gravity, which is the point at which its weight is spread.

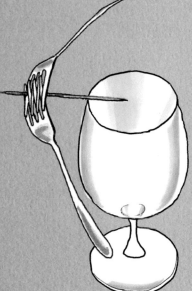

1 Take two forks and link the prongs together. This can be quite fiddly, so you might want to do this before you start the trick.

2 Push a toothpick through the middle of the prongs. Then balance the toothpick on the rim of a glass.

3 Once it's balanced, ask an adult to light a match and set light to the toothpick on the inside of the glass. It'll burn away, leaving the forks balancing on almost nothing!

Book friction

Take two equally sized books and interlace the pages so they overlap each other by about 5cm (2in). Give the books to a friend and ask them to try to pull them apart. It's almost impossible!

TOP TIP
The more pages that overlap, the better the trick will work. Spend a bit of time interlacing the pages.

Explore the Seven Wonders of the Ancient World

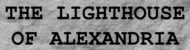

Ancient civilizations built many of the world's most **AMAZING SIGHTS**. As time has passed, other wonders have come and gone, but these seven are still considered to be among **THE GREATEST IN HISTORY**.

THE TEMPLE OF ARTEMIS AT EPHESUS

The temple, also known as the Temple of Diana, was built at Ephesus, Turkey, to honour Artemis, the Greek goddess of hunting. It was made of beautiful marble and was destroyed and rebuilt twice before finally being burnt down.

THE STATUE OF ZEUS AT OLYMPIA

This giant statue of the Greek God Zeus was built in Olympia, Greece. It was made of gold and ivory, and stood more than 12m (40ft) tall.

THE LIGHTHOUSE OF ALEXANDRIA

This lighthouse — the first one ever built — was one of the tallest designed and built structures on Earth for centuries.

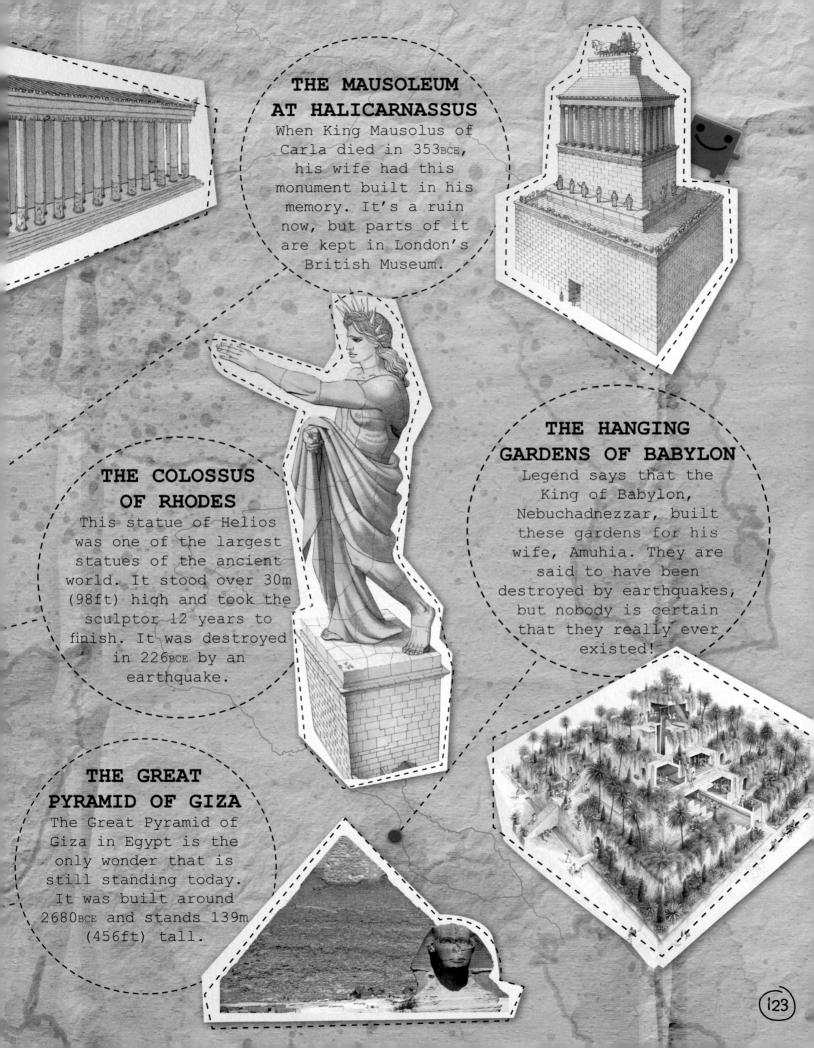

THE MAUSOLEUM AT HALICARNASSUS

When King Mausolus of Carla died in 353BCE, his wife had this monument built in his memory. It's a ruin now, but parts of it are kept in London's British Museum.

THE HANGING GARDENS OF BABYLON

Legend says that the King of Babylon, Nebuchadnezzar, built these gardens for his wife, Amuhia. They are said to have been destroyed by earthquakes, but nobody is certain that they really ever existed!

THE COLOSSUS OF RHODES

This statue of Helios was one of the largest statues of the ancient world. It stood over 30m (98ft) high and took the sculptor 12 years to finish. It was destroyed in 226BCE by an earthquake.

THE GREAT PYRAMID OF GIZA

The Great Pyramid of Giza in Egypt is the only wonder that is still standing today. It was built around 2680BCE and stands 139m (456ft) tall.

Glossary

Air pressure
The force exerted by the molecules in the air.

Animation
A sequence of images displayed quickly one after another to create the illusion of movement.

Bongos
A small set of drums played by hand.

Cacti
A type of spiny, usually leafless plant that often grows in deserts.

Chord
A group of musical notes played together to make a harmony.

Compass
A device that uses magnetism to find north.

Cooking measurements
The amount of each ingredient used in a recipe. Given in either metric or imperial units.

Craft mirror
A flexible material with a reflective surface.

Cutlass
A short sword with a curved blade that used to be common among sailors and pirates.

Disguise
A way of changing your appearance – usually with clothing – to hide your real identity.

Dough
A thick mixture of flour and liquid used to make bread, pizza, or pastry.

Equator
An imaginary line around the Earth that is equally distant from the north and south poles.

Fingerprint
A unique mark left on a surface or object caused by the oils on a person's fingertips.

Fossil
The remains of a prehistoric organism, such as a dinosaur skeleton, that have been preserved in the Earth.

Fret
A series of ridges on the neck of a guitar that create a particular sound when pressed at the same time a string is plucked or strummed.

Friction
The action of one surface rubbing against another.

Illusion
The act of deceiving a person by giving a false impression.

Molecule
A tiny, tiny piece of any substance. So small they're totally invisible to the naked eye.

NASA
The agency of the United Sates government responsible for spaceflight.

Non-Newtonian fluid
A substance that doesn't obey the usual laws of fluids, which behaves like a solid when pressure is applied to it.

Quinine
A chemical found in tonic water that glows when exposed to ultraviolet light.

Recycle
The act of reusing waste and turning it into something useful instead of throwing it away.

Safe
A secure container used to store valuable or important items.

Solar System
A collection of planets and their moons that orbit around a sun.

Songkran
A festival in Thailand to celebrate the New Year that is marked with the throwing of water

Squadron
A collection term for a group of aeroplanes.

Taste buds
The nerves in the tongue and mouth that are responsible for the sense of taste.

Theme
The central idea or subject of something. Usually a story, event, or setting.

Tonic water
A bitter tasting fizzy drink once used to protect against the disease Malaria.

UV (ultraviolet) light
A type of light that has a shorter wavelength than visible light.

Venom
A poisonous liquid used by animals such us snakes, spiders, and scorpions to kill or paralyze their predators or prey.

Xylophone
A musical instrument played by hitting a row of wooden or metal bars of varying lengths.

Yeast
A type of fungi used as an ingredient in baking to help bread and other foods rise.

Index

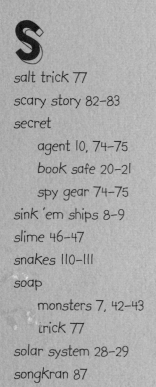
PICTURE CREDITS

The publisher would like to thank the following for their kind permission to reproduce their photographs:

(Key: a-above; b-below/bottom; c-centre; f-far; l-left; r-right; t-top)

62 Dorling Kindersley: Gary Kings - modelmaker (c). 63 Dorling Kindersley: Graham High at Centaur Studios - modelmaker (cr); Thomas Marent (cl); Gary Kings - modelmaker (bc). 77 Dorling Kindersley: Courtesy of Body Shop (cra, tc, tr). 84 Dorling Kindersley: Richard Chisolm / Pearson Education (bl). 91 PunchStock: Burke / Triolo Productions / Brand X (crb). 100 Dorling Kindersley: Courtesy of IFREMER, Paris (cb). 101 Dorling Kindersley: Courtesy of International Robotics (bc). Getty Images: Glowimages (tl). 111 Dorling Kindersley: Jerry Young (c).

All other images
© Dorling Kindersley
For further information see:
www.dkimages.com

DK WOULD LIKE TO THANK

Nikki Simms for proofreading, George Nimmo for production assistance, Sonia Charbonnier for technical assistance, and Romaine Werblow for image sourcing.